General Editor: M. Rolf Olsen

TAVISTOCK LIBRARY OF SOCIAL WORK PRACTICE

Intake Teams

Intake Teams

JOANNA BUCKLE

TAVISTOCK PUBLICATIONS
London and New York

First published in 1981 by
Tavistock Publications Ltd
11 New Fetter Lane, London EC4P 4EE
Published in the USA by
Tavistock Publications
in association with Methuen, Inc.
733 Third Avenue, New York, NY 10017

© 1981 Joanna Buckle
General editor's foreword © 1981 M. Rolf Olsen

Photoset by Rowland Phototypesetting Ltd
Bury St Edmunds, Suffolk
and printed in Great Britain by
Richard Clay (The Chaucer Press) Ltd
Bungay, Suffolk

British Library Cataloguing in Publication Data
Buckle, Joanna
Intake Teams. – (Tavistock library of social
work practice; SSP 220)
1. Public welfare – Great Britain
I. Title
361.4'0941   HV245

ISBN 0-422-77300-X
ISBN 0-422-77310-7 Pbk

Contents

General editor's foreword

Tavistock Library of Social Work Practice is a new series of books primarily written for practitioners and students of social work and the personal social services, but also for those who work in the allied fields of health, education, and other public services. The series represents the collaborative effort of social work academics, practitioners, and managers. In addition to considering the theoretical and philosophical debate surrounding the topics under consideration, the texts are firmly rooted in practice issues and the problems associated with the organization of the services. Therefore the series will be of particular value to undergraduate and post-graduate students of social work and social administration.

The series was prompted by the growth and increasing importance of the social services in our society. Until recently there has been a general approbation of social work, reflected in a benedictory increase in manpower and resources, which has led to an unprecedented expansion of the personal social services, a proliferation of the statutory duties placed upon them, and major reorganization. The result has been the emergence of a profession faced with the immense responsibilities of promoting individual and social betterment, and bearing a primary responsibility to advocate on behalf of individuals and groups who do not always fulfil or respect normal social expectations of behaviour. In spite of the growth in services these tasks are often carried out with inadequate resources, an uncertain knowledge base, and as yet unresolved difficulties associated with the reorganization of the personal social services in 1970. In recent years these difficulties have been compounded by a level of criticism unprecedented since the Poor Law. The anti-social-work critique has fostered some improbable alliances between groups of social administrators, sociologists, doctors, and the media, united in their belief that social work has failed in its general obligation to 'provide services to the people', and in its particular duty to socialize the delinquent, restrain parents who abuse their children, prevent old people from dying alone, and provide a satisfactory level of community care for the sick, the chronically handicapped, and the mentally disabled.

These developments highlight three major issues that deserve particular attention. First, is the need to construct a methodology for analysing social and personal situations and prescribing action; second, is the necessity to apply techniques that measure the performance of the individual worker and the profession as a whole in meeting stated objectives; third, and outstanding, is the requirement to develop a knowledge base against which the needs of clients are understood and decisions about their care are taken. Overall, the volumes in this series make explicit and clarify these issues; contribute to the search for the distinctive knowledge base of social work; increase our understanding of the aetiology and care of personal, familial, and social problems; describe and explore new techniques and practice skills; aim to raise our commitment towards low status groups which suffer public, political, and professional neglect, and to promote the enactment of comprehensive and socially just policies. Above all, these volumes aim to promote an understanding which interprets the needs of individuals, groups, and communities in terms of the synthesis between inner needs and the social realities that impinge upon them, and which aspire to develop informed and skilled practice.

M. ROLF OLSEN
Birmingham University
1981

Acknowledgements

Many people have played a part in the writing of this book from the time of my initial interest in intake work during my training, through my work in intake teams from the period when they were a new concept in social work, to today when they comprise an established part of the social work scene. To colleagues past and present I owe a great deal for their tolerance, enthusiasm, acceptance, and encouragement. Particularly I would like to thank colleagues and friends who have been members of the two intake teams of which I have been a part.

I would also like to record my debt to Rolf Olsen for his encouragement and support over the years, for his conviction that I could complete this work, and for his criticisms of the initial drafts.

Finally, both Marion Whitmell and Margaret Owers are to be congratulated on their valiant efforts in rendering my impossible handwriting into legible form.

Introduction

One of the major organizational innovations at area-team level in the decade after the reorganization of the personal social services along the lines laid down by the Seebohm Committee has been the establishment in many areas – counties, metropolitan districts, and London Boroughs – of intake teams. Conceived initially as an organizational response to the confusion that reigned in many of the new generic area teams after the establishment of unified social services departments, intake teams have been relatively slow to articulate explicitly their professional grounding, and hence to establish themselves as offering not only organizational and administrative, but also professional, advantages in handling new incoming work. Despite a flurry of articles on the establishment and development of intake teams in the first part of the 1970s, there has been little systematic discussion of the advantages and disadvantages of this model for the organization of area teams. Now that the dust of reorganization has settled, many area teams are once more examining their internal structuring and there is evidently a move towards considering alternatives to the basic intake/long-term division, particularly the development of patch teams and of specialist client-based teams.

In the light of this it is relevant to examine the historical origins of intake teams and the reasoning behind their development; their internal functioning and their relationship to other groups of workers in an area team; the nature of intake work, which has major implications for the work of departments as a whole; and the particular knowledge, skills, and theories of social work practice that are relevant to intake work. From an examination of these areas I would suggest that intake work qualifies as a specialism in its own right, and encompasses much of what the Seebohm Committee visualized as the new generic social work practice.

The establishment of intake teams in local authority social services departments as a means of organizing incoming work has served to highlight several issues that have hitherto been only implicitly acknowledged. When teams of workers are set up with a specific remit to handle new work presented to the department, they become the 'one door' through which virtually all requests for service must pass if they are to receive further attention. As such, intake workers act as gatekeepers for the services not only of their own department but also, in part, for the services of other agencies. With the increasing use of the social services department as a source of advice and information, the intake worker is in a key position to influence the flow of work to other agencies as well as to decide what is and what is not a proper case for the social services department. The roles of advocate and broker, increasingly being acknowledged as the province of the social worker, although relevant to social workers in diverse settings, are most often exercised at the point of intake, where many clients present with requests for help in negotiating with other departments and agencies, having been either unsuccessful themselves or overwhelmed by the apparent complexity of the task before them.

It is at intake that issues such as the role and function of a local authority social service department, the rationing of services, and the degree of priority afforded different requests for service are highlighted. It is also at the point of intake that departmental policy decisions on such matters are effected. It is, therefore, imperative that both the area team and the department are able to clearly state their objectives, priorities, and the ranking of priority, and that these are made explicit to staff who can then give a consistent response to the demands made upon them. Where no such clarity prevails, individual social workers – particularly intake workers – are left to respond to requests on an *ad hoc* basis and feel that they have to make subjective decisions on matters of rationing and priorities with little departmental support. The structural location of intake teams within the department, therefore, affords them a powerful role in determining the work of primarily the area team, but consequently also of the department as a whole. The location of such teams also means that potentially they are in a key position to identify newly emerging needs, once these begin to be presented to statutory agencies.

Given the great diversity of demands made on intake workers and the particular areas of work within which most intake work falls – that is, where the emphasis is on advice and information functions, assessment of problems presented, crisis work, and short-term intervention – the question arises as to whether intake work requires a different range of knowledge, expertise, and skills to that of social workers working to a more traditional long-term model of individual and family casework. An examination of the types of work under-taken by intake workers clearly shows that they require a vast range of knowledge, covering such areas as local resources, welfare rights, law, and departmental policies and procedures, in addition to social work theory and different models of practice to be able to function effectively and to the benefit of the client.

It is, therefore, arguable that there are particular areas of knowledge that are of special significance to intake work. Such areas include a working knowledge of legal and welfare rights, and a theoretical orientation towards crisis intervention and the various models of short-term and task-centred work. The structure of social work training needs to be better organized so as to both reflect, and enable training to contribute to, the realities of fieldwork in social services departments. Because the development of intake teams is one of the major innovations of the past decade in local-authority social work, training courses which ignore this area of work lack credibility in their avowed aims of preparing students for sub-sequent professional practice.

Over the past ten years intake work has emerged as one of the few specialist areas of work, including in its development the kind of generic work envisaged in the Seebohm Report. The question that now arises is whether such teams are an interim response to organizational change to be superseded by some new model of area-team organization, or whether they now constitute a specialist and lasting area of work, with its own particular range of skills, knowledge and expertise, and as such constitute a professional response yielding efficient and effective management of new work to the advantage of client, worker, and agency alike.

1

The arrival of unified social services departments

Introduction

During the 1960s pressure was mounting for a radical change in the organization of the personal social services. Many believed that the existing fragmentation, whereby different departments dealt with different client groups, had resulted in administrative overlapping, poor communication, uncoordinated activity, inefficiency, and a perplexing plethora of social work services. Against this background the Seebohm Committee was established to examine the existing structure and recommend changes. The recommendations, published in 1968, supported the unification of social services departments to replace the hitherto separate Children's, Welfare, and Mental Welfare Departments. Unified departments would, it was believed, provide an organizational structure most likely to be able to offer an efficient and effective family service with a community basis and preventive bias. The new social services departments were to provide an opportunity for a 'one-step' service – 'one-step' for clients to obtain a variety of services, and 'one-step' for social workers to serve simultaneously the different parties needing help.

Social services departments were consequently established in 1971 with the passing of the Local Authority Social Services Act. Social workers with different professional backgrounds, work experience, and social work skills and interests were now grouped together and expected to provide a generic social work service. The subsequent chaos and confusion that reigned in many departments was substantial. Not only were social workers unfamiliar with, and inexperienced in, many of the areas of work they were now expected to cover, but also the referral rate to the new departments rose dramatically in the early 1970s, both in the numbers and in the range of requests presented. One of the most positive and lasting innovations to arise directly from the Seebohm recommendations was the establishment of area teams to serve specified geographical areas. As a result of the pressures experienced by area teams, the impetus developed in some areas to look at new ways of internally structuring such teams, ultimately culminating in the development of intake teams, which can, therefore, be viewed as a direct consequence of Seebohm reorganization with its emphasis on the provision of a generic social work service at area-team level.

The background to reorganization in the personal social services

Today, when the specialist/generic debate in social work is still unresolved and there would appear to be a current trend towards increased specialization, there is a tendency to look back on the pre-Seebohm era as the halcyon days of specialization. Such a view is sometimes found within the profession, but there seems little doubt that from outside the structure of the service had relatively little to commend it. The British Medical Association, in their evidence to the Seebohm Committee, commented:

> 'The present fragmentation has caused inco-ordination of activity in the field and consequent duplication of effort and a risk of conflicting advice being offered, especially where departmental policies vary. This leads to confusion on both the part of the general practitioner and the public, who are often unsure to whom to refer patients or to whom to turn for advice. At present the selection of client and case worker is often more by chance than design, owing to the imprecise nature of the work and a lack of overall guidance. An all-purpose social welfare service could act as a clearing house in this respect and refer cases to the appropriate social worker.'
>
> (HMSO 1968: paragraph 510)

Seebohm himself, speaking in 1977, commented on the tendency to idealize the state of service, specialization, and expertise before 1971, adding: 'There is, I am afraid, a certain nostalgia for the cosy and smaller departments with clearly defined duties, but leaving so many needs unmet' (Seebohm 1977: 11).

The roots of the local authority personal social services are to be found primarily in the Poor Law, although the voluntary sector, both independently and in conjunction with the local authority, has always played a major role. Services developed on an *ad hoc* and piecemeal basis in response to specific problems as they arose and made an impact on the public consciousness, which then required some provision to be made. Different categories of need were gradually being separated off before 1948, culminating in 1948 in the duties of local authority public assistance committees being divided between two new local authority departments, one responsible for children and the other for welfare. The National Assistance Board became responsible for functions of financial assistance and income maintenance. Indeed, as the Report comments: 'throughout the break up of the Poor Law a key factor was the conviction that cerain groups had special needs, which demanded special treatment surpassing what was or could be offered by an all-purpose Poor Law system' (HMSO 1968: paragraph 52).

It would therefore be fair to say that in 1948 the organization of the personal social services changed from the generic system of the Poor Law to an organizational system based on specialist services, separately organized, for different and quite specifically defined groups. The personal social services provided by the local authority were located primarily in: the Children's Department, which was responsible for the care and welfare of deprived children and, after the Children and Young Persons Act 1963, undertook preventive work; the Welfare Department, which was responsible for providing accommodation and other services to the elderly, physically handicapped, and homeless families; and the local authority health department, which was responsible for the mentally ill and mentally handicapped in addition to their responsibilities held before 1948 for providing domestic help to lying-in mothers and, later, to the sick and infirm. Social work elements were also present in the work of Health departments with the chronically sick, in Education departments with the development of educational welfare services, and in

Housing departments in housing welfare functions. This structure was set up after the Second World War and was not comprehensively reviewed until the Seebohm Committee started meeting in 1966. The committee was then faced with: 'a variety of services which are not only fragmented in terms of departmental responsibility and objectives but are also at different stages of development' (HMSO 1968: paragraph 56). Such diversity obviously implied difficulties in coordination, both at management level in terms of policy and planning, and at fieldwork level in the day-to-day management and decision making in the handling of individual cases.

Traditionally, social work has been organized along the following lines: specialization by client group (the elderly, the physically handicapped, the mentally ill, children, etc); specialization as a result of the location of work (hospital, court, etc.); or specialization by method (group work, community work, etc.). In Britain during the 1950s and 1960s specialization by client group was the over-riding focus for the organization and practice of social work, and this became further entrenched as a result of statutory duties laid down by post-war legislation. This resulted in a somewhat piecemeal approach, responding to individuals on the basis of the client group they were classified into, rather than the problem for which they were seeking help. Furthermore, it militated against the recognition of the interrelatedness of difficulties in families, paying scant regard to the individual's family and wider social circumstances.

Take, for example, a three-generation family where the mental and physical health of the grandmother was deteriorating. The strain on the daughter of caring for her sick mother was considerable and she became very short-tempered, irritable, and inconsistent in the handling of her own two young children, who were then considered to be at risk. Such a family could conceivably have been involved with all three departments on different aspects of their family problem. Each worker would be focusing on the symptom/problem of the individual family member for whom they had responsibility but it is clear that without an overview of the family's problems, prevention of breakdown, even if seen as an objective, would be unlikely while different workers, each with a different focus, were involved.

Although the lack of a family-oriented service in the 1950s and 1960s resulted in a paucity of preventive work, some Children's

Departments had begun to establish 'family caseworkers' to assume a somewhat wider brief in working with 'problem families'. In the voluntary field the family had long been the focus for social work endeavour. The Family Welfare Association was established in Victorian times and stood for the fostering and development of family life, and the encouragement of self-help by the family and community. Family Service Units, the successors in 1948 to the Pacifist Service Units established by a number of conscientious objectors during the war, saw one of their objects as to undertake intensive and comprehensive welfare work with families unable to maintain adequate standards without special assistance, and advocated employing a range of staff, including social workers, teachers, doctors, nurses, psychologists, and psychiatrists, towards this end.

The organization and specialization of social work in terms of client group belies another feature of social work practice particularly evident in the 1950s and 1960s: the concentration on the individual. Social work emerged against the background of Poor Law relief in the Victorian era, when poverty and destitution were seen largely as a result of personal failings. Gradually over the years, and with the increasing range of state provision of welfare services, social handicap came to be recognized as at least in part a product of the interaction between the individual and his environment. Despite this shift in emphasis, however, social work was, and largely remains, geared towards maximizing the private resources – emotional, material, and intellectual – of the individual within the family. Social work practice has developed throughout this century primarily in relation to meeting individual need, and until the early 1970s focused heavily on the area of individual pathology, seeing problems as intra-personal in origin and requiring 'treatment' by skilled casework. From the 1920s the American style of social work with its emphasis on the use of Freudian concepts and psychoanalytic models became one of the leading forces in British social work training and practice, culminating in the identification of casework with 'the art of changing human attitudes' (Wooton 1978: 14). Consequently, 'skilled casework' came to be seen as the *sine qua non* of British social work practice, as a method of 'treatment' for individuals who were encountering any variety of problems, whether they be of an emotional, financial, marital, or physical nature.

Casework was invariably viewed as a long-term process, and hence even in the 1960s long-term casework intended to bring about major changes in the client and his way of life was regarded as the desirable norm. Short-term work with limited goals was seen as 'not quite proper'.

This attitude has long hindered the development of effective short-term work and encouraged the continuation of a practice of watered-down and often ill-conceived psycho-analysis. The Brunel team (Social Services Organizational Research Unit 1974), in their work on social services departments, discuss the structure of the 'Applications Sector' found in some Children's Departments, set up to deal with all new work – a forerunner in a specialist department of the intake teams found in area teams today. In their description of the functioning of such a system, they mention that child care officers in the applications sector also carried a small case load to allow them to develop other skills and keep them in touch with the general work of the agency. The clear implication seems to be that the short-term and crisis work undertaken by staff in dealing with and assessing new cases is not 'real' social work and stands apart from the proper work of the agency, probably thereby being awarded a lower status than the ideal 'long-term casework' model.

Social work in the local authorities before 1971 therefore consisted basically of social workers working in separate and specialist departments, organized on the basis of the client group served. Problems were dealt with on an individual basis with little attention to their wider origins or ramifications, being thought of largely as intra-personal dysfunctioning that should be properly treated by long-term casework. The effects of this system of organization on staff and the public varied. Social workers working in separate departments were organized to achieve the specific objectives of those departments rather than to meet the full range of the client's needs. Social workers, therefore, worked to an apparently fairly clearly defined system where limit setting was reasonably clear in terms of what was or was not a particular department's responsibility.

However, such a system was widely open to abuse and buck-passing between departments; for example, in terms of what is the 'real' problem. To return to our three-generation family, is it the grandmother's physical handicap, mother's mental illness, or the need for the children to be received into care that is the 'real' problem? The family could be passed between the Welfare, Mental Welfare, and Children's Departments in a never-ending vicious circle, because each Department deals with only one part of the family and sees the major responsibility as that of another department. The employment of social workers by separate departments with their own objectives and client-group orientation had advantages in that it gave workers both a clear sense of professional identity – as evidenced by the existence of a range of professional organizations such as the Association of Child Care Officers, Institute of Medical Social Workers, and the Association of Psychiatric Social Workers – and the opportunity to develop specialist knowledge and skills in a defined area of work, resulting in increased confidence on the part of the worker and a better service to the client. However, set against such advantages was the shortage of resources, including trained manpower, the high numbers of cases in workers' caseloads, and the lack of research on social work effectiveness.

Although the existence of separate departments had some advantages for the social workers employed, there was little to recommend such organization to clients. The pattern of service was often unclear, as was the division of responsibilities between them. In the circumstances where the client or referrer was either unable to clearly articulate their need, or where the need was unclear (for it may need skilled assessment to unravel the various strands of a problem) it would often be difficult to get directly to the right service and there were some needs for which no service had a clearly defined responsibility. In addition, newly recognized and newly emergent needs, resulting from social change, were not catered for; nor did any department have a particular responsibility to investigate such new areas of work – for example, problems particular to immigrant families. Even where the problem was a fairly straightforward one centralized offices, poor reception facilities, and lack of public information about available services and how to apply for them made the applicant's route hazardous. Such difficulties of access to services were equally bemusing to other agencies who had cause to refer clients, such as general practitioners, hospitals, the Supplementary Benefits Commission, and voluntary organizations. The net result of such access problems was that clients or other referral agents became frustrated and disheartened and did not refer.

The Seebohm Committee was appointed on 20 December 1965: 'to review the organization and responsibilities of the local authority personal social services in England and Wales, and to consider what changes are desirable to secure an effective family service' (HMSO 1968: paragraph 1). At the time there was dissatisfaction with the way services were being provided and in particular growing public concern at the increase in juvenile crime. Numerous bodies, both official and unofficial, were preparing reports that included suggestions on the prevention of crime and the treatment of young offenders. The culmination was the presentation to Parliament in August 1965 of the White Paper 'The Child, The Family and the Young Offender'. This set out the Government's proposals to revise the law and practice relating to offenders under the age of 21, and its proposals for practical reforms to support the family and to forestall and reduce delinquency. The line was clearly drawn between the functioning of the family unit and the effect of this on the occurrence of delinquency. There was, therefore, a shift of emphasis away from the individual and towards seeing him in his social (in this case family) context. The inherent social value of the family was recognized, and the importance of working to reduce the risk of family breakdown was seen as relevant to the prevention of delinquency.

Since 1948 there had been considerable expansion in the field of social services, and changes both in how needs were conceptualized and in strategies for meeting them. Legislation had extended the powers and duties conferred on local authorities, such as The Mental Health Act 1959 and The Children and Young Persons Act 1963. The latter Act had a major effect on the Seebohm Committee in that it established in legislation the importance of preventive work. The Children's Act 1948, upon which the children's service was based, obliged local authorities to appoint children's officers whose duty it was to restore to their families children who had been received into care. Although a logical extension of such a duty was to work towards the prevention of family breakdown in the first place, thereby obviating the need for reception into care, it was not until the Children and Young Persons Act 1963 that the duties of the local authority were extended and prevention made an explicit objective. Under Section 1 of this Act the local authority was required to make available: 'such advice, guidance and assistance as may promote the welfare of children by diminishing the need to receive children into or keep them in care . . . or to bring children before a juvenile court'. This was not merely an empty altruistic goal but was reinforced by the establishment of a provision to help families financially where such financial assistance would prevent the need for reception into care. In addition, whilst the Seebohm Committee was sitting two other major pieces of legislation were on their way into the statute books: the Children and Young Persons Act 1969 and the Chronically Sick and Disabled Persons Act 1970.

These Acts laid more extensive duties on local authorities for the provision of services both to children and the handicapped. More than this, they embodied the emerging philosophy of the State reaching out to seek those people in need in the community, rather than dealing solely with unavoidable social casualties. There was also strong central government pressure to hasten the expansion of community care. Institutional care became increasingly unpopular and greater emphasis was placed on the desirability of care for a wide range of disadvantaged individuals in the community. Consequently movement became apparent between institutions and the community – for example, in the discharge of long-stay psychiatric patients. For such policies to achieve any degree of success a high degree of collaboration and co-ordination is required between different departments, for clearly the individual cared for in the community will require a wider range of diverse services than when he is placed in an institution. Furthermore, the family with a handicapped or disturbed member living with them are likely to require support and services of a different kind to those needed if he were accommodated elsewhere. Central-government-inspired policies, therefore, such as the development and encouragement of community-care programmes emphasized the difficulties and problems of co-ordination and collaboration between fragmented departments.

There were, then, two major conceptual advances that formed a background to the work of the Seebohm Committee: the desire to provide an effective family service, and the new emphasis on the role and importance of preventive work. The level of knowledge and understanding of social need was becoming much greater and more sophisticated, and the realization of the complexity of such need highlighted the interrelatedness of many different factors and the desirability of developing a comprehensive approach. The problems of co-ordination and collaboration between the varied strands of the personal social services as they were then organized consequently posed a major dilemma. The services, organized along divisions on the basis of age, problem, or legal/adminstrative classification, took little account of the family as a whole, its corporate existence, or the fact that some individuals faced a series of interrelated problems for which different services may be responsible. There was evident 'a growing desire to treat both the individual and the family as a whole and to see them in their wider social contexts' (HMSO 1968: paragraph 79), which accentuated difficulties of co-ordination both at policy and field levels.

Similarly, the increasing move towards, and interest in, undertaking preventive work 'involves a broader view of social and individual problems than the present structure of services easily permits, and often demands considerable collaboration between several organizations and professions'. This growing emphasis on the family as the prime focus for the organization of services caused the Committee to consider what unit it was actually concerned with, that is, the vexed question of: 'What is a family?' This question is dealt with early in the Report and the breadth of the answer may well be seen as one of the major stumbling blocks of the later social services departments. In reply to the question 'What is a family?' the Report says: 'We decided very early in our discussions that it would be impossible to restrict our work solely to the needs of two- or even three-generation families. We could only make sense of our task by considering also childless couples and individuals without any close relatives: in other words, everybody' (HMSO 1968: paragraph 32).

The establishment of such a broad-ranging social service aimed at locating problems at an early enough stage that prevention becomes a realistic goal is dependent upon identification of areas of need. A preventive social service, therefore, requires an adequate forecasting of changing social needs. Social changes during the 1950s and 1960s served to highlight the deficiencies of the existing organization, for many of the newly emergent problem areas were either covered inadequately or not at all. Three obvious areas of work where there was a significant growth in need not matched by an increase in, or diversification of, resources were the growth in the proportion of the population who were members of ethnic minorities; the ageing of the population; and the increased demand for a childminding service as more and more women with children sought employment. The personal social services as they were constituted were not considered to be sufficiently flexible to meet such changes in the nature and extent of social need, and it was felt necessary to work towards better forecasting of developing needs, alongside the establishment of a system of organization with sufficient flexibility to be able to adapt rapidly to meet such needs.

The Seebohm Committee believed that there was a growing sense of dissatisfaction with the local authority personal social services and that this centred primarily around three major issues: inadequacies in the amount of provision, inadequacies in the range of provision, and inadequacies in the quality of provision. Local authorities were found to be not fully meeting the needs for which they had a clear responsibility, as evidenced by the waiting lists for various kinds of day and residential provision for such groups as the elderly and mentally ill, and also by the shortfall of supply of domiciliary services such as home help and meals on wheels. The fragmented nature of the existing services left some needs, or groups of people for which no service had a clearly defined responsibility, highlighted by newly recognized or emergent problems which fell into none of the conventionally defined categories. Finally the quality of the services provided also came in for criticism; lack of time, staff, and training being held responsible for the low standards found in some areas. The inadequate quality of service is closely related to what was seen as a lack of relevant knowledge about many social problems and consequent uncertainty about what form of provision would be most appropriate. Neither central government nor local government were accepting the responsibility to organize the systematic collection and sharing of data and information upon which research into more effective service provision could be based.

Once again the fragmentation of the organization of the personal social services was viewed as the root of many of these dissatisfactions. Responsibility for development of policy, use of resources, setting of priorities, and issues of public accessibility, accountability, and co-ordination was divided between different departments. The more the responsibility for the provision of services became divided the more pronounced were the problems. Different departments would plan, set priorities, and develop their own policies in an insular fashion, with little co-ordination amongst themselves, although all worked in interrelated fields. Little regard was paid to the implications plans made in one department would have for another.

Similar problems were acknowledged both in Europe and in the United States in the 1960s. Although the administrative, political, and geographical features of different countries varied enormously there were remarkable similarities in their organizational problems in the field of personal social services. Two common features emerged. Firstly, there was a deficiency in co-ordination between the various social agencies and a consequent less than adequate service to individuals and families and an inefficient deployment of resources. Secondly, the accessibility of such services was often considered poor and remote with little involvement of community or consumer. Indeed, Cooper (1978) comments in looking back over the past decade in social services that the old distinctive and separated services seem irrelevant to post-industrial society which, for social and economic reasons, is producing not only traditional stresses but developing new ones.

The Seebohm Committee was, therefore, confronted with the task of examining the range of personal social services as they were then organized and considering whether a change in organizational structure would deliver a more comprehensive service to all elements in the population, overcoming the divisive and compartmentalized pattern of service delivery that then existed, with the goal of providing a pattern for an effective family service which would work at a preventive level. Such expectations, taken together with the emerging philosophy of the personal social services reaching out to those in need, laid the foundations for the legendary ideal that all problems could be checked if not avoided and that 'everyone' could be maintained within the community.

The aims and objectives of Seebohm reorganization

The Seebohm Committee set itself three central questions: what was wrong with the current organization of the personal social services and what improvements could be made; if improvements were to be made were these dependent on organizational changes and consequent changes in the division of responsibility; and finally, what new pattern should be recommended? (HMSO 1968: paragraph 71). The pattern that finally emerged, the establishment of social services departments, arose out of what the Committee saw as the clear need for reorganization to fulfil what they viewed as the aims and objectives of the local authority social services. Reorganization was seen as the means towards improvement in service in order to meet the overall needs of the family or individual, provide a clear and comprehensive pattern of responsibility and accountability, attract more resources, use those resources more effectively, generate adequate recruitment and training of staff, meet needs currently being neglected, adapt to changing conditions, provide for better data collection and dissemination, and be more accessible and comprehensible to the public. The overriding consideration was the desire to organize in such a way as to provide an effective family service that would, apparently, cover the whole population from the cradle to the grave. The assumption was that much of the day-to-day work of the social services departments would be the provision of general family guidance, and that the proposed organizational change would facilitate such provision.

The object of much of this family guidance was to be directed towards the prevention of social distress, to minimize human suffering and family breakdown. Prevention, however, is dependent on knowledge about what action really is preventive; the ability to recognize at an early stage those individuals, families, or groups most at risk; and (even given the former two conditions) the extent to which the agency has the capacity in terms of time, staff, and resources to provide a service other than on a 'casualty' basis. Preventive action, moreover, functions on two levels. 'Primary' or 'general' prevention comprises action that is directed towards preventing social problems, such as community-wide policies aimed at creating an environment conducive to social well-being. 'Secondary' or 'specific' prevention comprises action designed to catch problems at an early enough stage so that it is possible to either reverse them or at least prevent deterioration or recurrence. Such services are generally focused on specific individuals, families, or groups.

The personal social services, with their traditional emphasis on the symptoms of the individual, when able to move beyond the 'casualty' service towards emphasis on preventive work, worked mainly in the field of 'secondary' or 'specific' prevention. Help was, therefore, to be directed towards individuals and families who were recognized to be at particular risk, and where the problems were likely to generate further and more profound difficulties unless some intervention was made. The likely success of such preventive work depends on sufficiently early recognition of the problem and referral to social services as well as the availability of adequate resources. Such early identification is dependent upon the development of trust and adequate systems of communication between different agencies. General practitioners, health visitors, teachers, housing officials, and social security officers, for example, are all likely to be in contact with families with problems, whereas such families are often not known to social workers until they are referred, often in crisis or at a stage when problems have become entrenched and are unlikely to be so amenable to social work intervention. The Seebohm Committee realized the importance of such inter-agency co-operation, and the responsibility of the local authority as a whole as well as the social services department to demonstrate what it can usefully achieve in the area of preventive work to secure appropriate and realistic referrals rather than to become the dumping ground for the intractable problems of all other agencies.

'Primary' or 'general' preventive action is largely the concern of central government in terms of the development of universal services or policies designed to reduce the levels of social and economic distress throughout the community. Adequate personal social services are dependent upon such factors as adequate housing, health care, and income. However, within local authorities there are often specific geographical areas of comprehensive high risk. Such areas are often the social consequence of factors such as large-scale urban development, employment mobility, the growth of new housing estates, the increasing number of immigrants in urban areas, and the persistent deprivation of some neighbourhoods. Community work began to develop from the mid-1950s onwards in response to the problems caused by such factors. During the 1950s the London Council of Social Service pioneered work with already existing groups such as tenants associations, giving direct help and encouragement and acting as a provider of information, and a mediator with other groups, including the local authority. The inherent conflicts and power struggles which came to be the focus of community work during the 1960s and 1970s was little in evidence during the 1950s. The 1960s, however, saw a dramatic increase in the incidence of self-help groups, such as playgroups, squatters groups, and tenants associations. The Seebohm Committee saw their proposals for reorganization as, at a higher level, embodying a wider conception of social service:

> 'directed to the well-being of the whole of the community and not only of social casualties and seeing the community it serves as a basis of its authority, resources and effectiveness. Such a conception spells, we hope, the death knell of the Poor Law legacy and the socially divisive attitudes and the practices which stemmed from it.'
>
> (HMSO 1968: paragraph 474)

The Committee, therefore, saw several services as having a role to play not only at the 'secondary' or 'specific' level of prevention but also at the 'primary' or 'general' level and identified:

> 'the need for the personal social services to engage in the extremely difficult and complex task of encouraging and assisting the development of community identity and mutual aid, particularly in areas characterized by rapid population turnover, high delinquency, child deprivation and mental illness rates and other indices of social pathology. Social work with individuals alone is bound to be of limited effect in an area where the community environment itself is a major impediment to healthy individual development.'
>
> (HMSO 1968: paragraph 477)

To pursue this preventive work at the community level, a new area of work for previously personal social services, the necessity of investigating the needs of the area and for the co-ordination and collaboration of services and resources both in the voluntary and statutory fields, became clear. Effective co-ordination with other agencies and the mobilization of community resources were seen as important since: 'The staff of the social service department will need to see themselves not as a self-contained unit but as a part of a network of services within the community' (HMSO 1968: paragraph 478). The objective, therefore, was not solely an effective family service, but one that was community-orientated, encouraging maximum participation of individuals and groups in the community in the planning, organization, and provision of social services.

Despite the fact that even before the mid-1960s many social work training courses claimed to be generic in their design and content, because of the organizational structure of the personal social services most social workers started their training with the expectation that they would work in a specialized department, as a child care officer, mental welfare officer, medical or psychiatric social worker, or social welfare officer, and there was relatively little movement across departmental boundaries. This was in part accounted for by the lack of opportunity for training, resulting in most staff having to depend on their practical work experience and the consequent unreadiness of different departments to employ them. The Seebohm Committee rejected suggestions that social workers could either continue to work on much the same basis as in the separate departments, or that they continue to be employed to work with specific categories of people after a common generic training course. They preferred that there should be common training courses in social work and that the pattern of employment with specialized groups should be radically altered. This preference was dictated primarily by the ideal espoused by the Committee that an individual or family in need of help from the social services should be served as far as possible by a single social worker. Such a single worker would then be in a better position to meet the needs of the individual or family as a whole, rather than in the fragmentary fashion that was previously often the case. Furthermore, there would be less confusion about issues of responsibility and accountability. It was recognized that there may be some problems where other social workers, perhaps with more specialist skills, may need to be involved – for example, in marital work, or work with disturbed adolescents – but such inclusion of other workers was seen to be the result of decisions made by the social worker primarily responsible – the forerunner of the concept of the key worker. The Committee envisaged that basic-grade social workers would be generically trained and undertake a wide range of social work functions. Specialization was viewed as necessary above basic-grade level, and would often require further training. Social workers with specialized knowledge would act as consultants and may well be based centrally within the local authority, rather than in area teams. The Committee comments: 'the kind of social worker we expect to emerge will be one who has had a generic training specially aimed at giving him competence, after experience, to cope with a whole range of social need, provided he has the support of adequate consultation and other resources' (HMSO 1968: paragraph 527).

Therefore, the Seebohm Committee's intent was quite clearly that social workers should not only be generically trained but would be expected to practise across the field of social need, dealing with the whole range of work that came under the auspices of the previously divided departments as well as at individual, family, group, and community levels. Such breathtakingly broad expectations have coloured the practice of social work for the past decade, causing a deep divide between those that espouse the cause of generic practice and those who see it as leading to a dilution of skills and knowledge available to the client, and therefore a lowering of standards of professional practice. Some have argued that the Committee's aim was to introduce generic teams – specialist workers together forming a team with skills covering all areas of practice – rather than to introduce individual generic workers, but it seems clear from the Report that the latter was the explicit aim. This could well have arisen out of what may now be considered to be an overreaction to the rigid classification implied by the pre-Seebohm symptom-orientated approach by divided departments.

For generic workers to provide a service that was community based, the Seebohm Committee had to consider the organization of fieldwork within the proposed unified social services department. For the service provided to be effective in terms of the population it served, it had to be both accessible and acceptable, and be so organized as to promptly meet the needs presented to it. The recurring complaint presented to the Committee was that the personal social services were housed and located in a way which was often a deterrent to potential users. Offices were usually situated in local government complexes in the centre of towns, were often forbidding in atmosphere, and reception facilities were poor. The Committee, therefore, proposed that to achieve a high degree of effectiveness coupled with the aim of a community based service, social work teams should be based in area offices. No standard pattern was proposed, as in each area much depended on the availability of suitable staff and premises. Initial suggestions were that in towns, an area office might serve a population of 50,000–100,000 with a minimum of 10–12 social workers. The size of the area, population served, and kind of organization adopted would depend very heavily on the different patterns of need in different areas, variations in the age distribution of the population being particularly relevant.

The Committee recognized that it was unlikely to be possible to provide area offices on the necessary scale to be readily available to the whole population until some time in the future, and suggested that, in the meantime: 'in addition to the provision of advice and information at the area office, the social service department may well need to establish (either itself or in conjunction with other agencies including voluntary agencies) more widely distributed advice and information centres in specific sub-areas, neighbourhoods, and communities' (HMSO 1968: paragraph 593). The predecessor of this has been in the different forms of family advice centres set up by some Children's Departments after the impetus given to preventive work by the Children and Young Persons Act 1963. However, the Committee clearly viewed the social services department as an information and advice agency as well as a social work agency.

To summarize, the aims and objectives of the Seebohm Committee's report was to set up a unified social services department which would provide a broadly based effective family service on a community basis, operating from area offices which would be easily accessible to the public. The concept behind this was one of a humane service reaching out to individuals, groups, and communities to help troubled people gain a measure of control over their own lifestyles and destinies, and informed by notions of locality, reciprocity, and the need for flexibility in response to changing needs. A major industry was created to distribute 'human services' and the need for these services, to which there was to be universal accessibility, would be determined by professional judgement rather than by fixed criteria laid out in a rule book. The Committee made no formal statement on the proper aims of social services departments, while implying extremely wide-sweeping aims of an unspecific nature, related to the alleviation of social distress. Moreover, the Committee made no attempt to organize a research programme based on its plans for reorganization, on the grounds that any research programme would be too complex and time consuming and was unlikely to produce clear and reliable results.

Neither the Committee nor the new departments subsequently set up, therefore, had adequate data for service planning, and consequently the amount of unmet need and articulated demand that appeared after reorganization did so with explosive force on unsuspecting social services departments. Furthermore, the Report, presented at a time of relative economic expansion, paid scant attention to the financial implications of its proposals, apparently assuming unlimited expansion on all fronts.

The effects of reorganization immediately after the Seebohm Report

'The Seebohm reorganization at the beginning of this decade stuck together a tradition of watery psycho-analysis, legal duties, and more straightforward welfare provision, called the lot a profession, and made its practitioners employees of local authorities which don't reckon much at all to the tradition of professional autonomy. No social glue can make that lot altogether coherent, the wonder is that it bears stress as well as it does.'

(Shearer 1979)

The initial response to the Seebohm Report was euphoric, with a rapid rise in expectations on the part of practitioners, and in demand by consumers. The newly formed unified social services departments were confronted with a huge increase in demand for service, and there was consequently a tremendous rise in staff numbers, from 17,500 in 1972 to 24,400 in 1975 (Seebohm 1977). The social services department became the local bureaucracy with the human face, with a shift of emphasis from officials administering the regulations to social workers giving a professional service. Eligibility for service became, in theory, a matter for professional assessment and decision. When the expectations of both the public and the profession alike were not fulfilled, the result was dissatisfaction and frustration.

With the advent of the unified social services departments, staff with a wide variety of backgrounds, training, and experience were thrown together and then divided into geographically based teams, rather than teams organized by client group served, which had previously been the case. Although each of these new teams had a specific geographical area for which they were responsible, in many authorities the Seebohm ideal of area teams, located within the geographical area which they were to serve, was a long time in coming. This delay was due to such factors as lack of suitable premises, and consequently many area teams were to remain centrally based for some time. Even within the old specialist departments there had been specialized areas of work; for example, welfare officers dealing specifically with the blind or deaf in the Welfare Departments, child care officers specializing in adoption in the Children's Departments, or mental welfare officers with particular knowledge, skill, and expertise in dealing with the mentally handicapped in the Mental Welfare Departments. All workers in 1971, therefore, were specialists in one area of work, some with more narrowly circumscribed knowledge and skills than others. As a result of reorganization all social workers were confronted with the expectation that they would be able to respond to a wide spectrum of human need, dealing with areas of work where they often had no knowledge or experience, let alone training. Welfare officers used to dealing with the blind were faced with parents demanding reception of children into care, ex-mental-welfare officers with non-accidentally injured children, and ex-child-care officers with the possibility of an individual needing compulsory admission to a psychiatric hospital. Whilst in allocating staff to geographical areas there was generally an attempt to organize things such that there were members from each of the previously separate departments in the area team, it was often the case that, for example, those staff with child-care experience were out of the office when a child-care crisis arose, leaving staff experienced in a different field to make decisions and take action. Area teams made up of a range of different specialist workers expected to continue to concentrate on their own specialism constituted an interpretation of Seebohm's drive for a generic service as meaning the establishment of generic teams rather than generic workers.

However, because there was now only one agency for all referrals, area teams organized in this way also required – to offer an efficient and effective service to new clients who may require immediate advice, assistance, or action – front-line workers who possessed knowledge and skills across the whole range of work the social services departments now encompassed: that is, front-line generic workers. Furthermore, as a result of the rapid increase in the numbers of staff employed, there arose a pattern of rapid promotion in order to fill line-management posts. Some individuals were employed as senior social workers with very little (and in some cases none at all) post-qualification fieldwork experience. Despite Seebohm's espousal of professional consultants with specialist post-qualification training, to act as a resource for basic-grade generic fieldworkers, the reality was one of senior social workers acting primarily as social-service managers, often with limited fieldwork experience or specialist knowledge. Such career hunting, though understandable since the new departments obviously required managers, left clients having to deal with a rapid succession of social workers, rather than benefiting from the continuity offered by one social worker over a long period; and social workers experienced reduced job satisfaction as a result of rapid staff turnover, and very limited access to expert advice.

At the time of reorganization staff were, naturally, prone to many fantasies about 'those other people', the staff from different departments, and there was generally a hostility and unwillingness towards building up a generic case load. Traditional patterns of agency loyalty and professional identity were broken down, and it took considerable time, and developments in area-team organizational patterns, to achieve some unity of purpose in staff with hitherto different outlooks and loyalties. Neill *et al.* (1976), in a study of the different perceptions of social workers in four area offices between 1972 and 1975, comments on the sense of impotence and inefficiency felt by social workers suddenly being expected to offer a generic service. The initial response of social work staff was to keep, as far as possible, a specialist case load; that is, those types of cases they would have dealt with before reorganization. In 1972 two out of three fieldworkers were classified as specialist or semi-specialist (carrying a case load where over 75 per cent of cases were of one type of problem), whereas by 1975 this had reduced to one in three. Similarly in 1972 80 per cent of child-care cases were part of specialist case loads, whereas by 1975 50 per cent of child-care cases were part of mixed case loads. Most social workers in 1972 were apprehensive about taking on new work, possessive about their specialization, and had little trust in the ability and interest of others in taking on new areas of work; the majority thought specialization would continue indefinitely, and preferred this. Reorganization and the consequent wide-ranging expectations laid on basic-grade field-workers resulted initially in a lowering of morale, a loss of confidence, and consequent increases in felt anxiety and stress owing to the unfamiliar roles social workers were called upon to fulfil.

The dramatic increase in the number of referrals to social services departments after reorganization imposed yet further external pressures on the service, already struggling with the wide range of internal difficulties that had arisen out of the reorganized structure. Various factors seem to have played a part in the increase of work coming in to departments after the Seebohm reorganization. The new unified departments uncovered, almost unwittingly, a huge reservoir of unmet need arising out of new legislation and increased public expectations, which culminated not only in an increase in the net volume of demands being presented, but also in an increase in the variety of these demands. Individuals for whom no department had previously acknowledged any responsibility now came within the auspices of the umbrella-like social services departments. In addition the recent enactment of such legislation as The Children and Young Persons Act 1969 and The Chronically Sick and Disabled Persons Act 1970 coupled with the strong central government pressure to hasten the advent of programmes of community care all placed wider responsibilities on the shoulders of the newly formed social services departments. There had been a general increase in social problems such as juvenile delinquency, the numbers of elderly in the population, and the rate of marital breakdown, further increasing the potential demands made on social services departments; finally, somewhat greater public awareness of the existence of social services departments in the wake of publicity about the reorganization had led to unrealistic expectations on the part of the public, and increased dissatisfaction at the discovery that resources available lagged behind the level of expectation.

Given these pressures – particularly the added commitments resulting from new legislation at a time when social workers were trying to adjust to large, new, generic departments – some have felt that survival itself was an achievement, and that the increased

demands delayed the cohesion and effectiveness of the new departments. The mushrooming of the social services departments, as
evidenced by the increase in social services expenditure as a
percentage of total public expenditure from 0.5 per cent in 1953 to
0.8 per cent in 1968, and 1.6 per cent in 1974 (Personal Social
Services Council 1976), had the effect of encouraging other agencies
to refer cases to social services more than before, which was also
perhaps the result of having only one unified, as opposed to several
disparate, departments to approach.

Another major factor relating to the increase in referrals after
reorganization, and colouring much of the subsequent development
of local authority social work over the past decade, has been the
question of boundaries. The Seebohm Committee never spelt out
the proper aims of social services departments, but by various
means they assured that there were effectively no limits to the role of
local authority social services: by deciding that no individual could
be excluded, in discussing the question of the definition of a family;
by extending the range of work to include a community basis as well
as work with individuals and families; and by stressing the importance of preventive work as opposed to working solely in areas
where the department had statutory responsibilities. The social
services departments were ready to accept all burdens, they had no
boundaries, and as a result of the lack of research carried out by the
Seebohm Committee and their relative ignorance of the financial
implications of their Report, no measurements to warn the departments of the overdrafts with which they were to be confronted. The
breadth of the comprehensive approach advocated by the Seebohm
Committee both affected the expectations of the public and caused
social work to be seen as making great claims that it could not then
fulfil. Given that the span of activities that was seen as the proper
area of work for social services departments was so broad as to feel at
times virtually limitless, other agencies felt free to unload their
problem cases onto the social services departments. Many of the
problems landing at the door of the new departments were virtually
intractable, and when little or nothing could be achieved the result
was often criticism of social services. All this resulted in a blurred
image of social work, and the public could hardly be blamed for
being unclear about the functions of the new departments, since
many staff had little clearer a notion. This lack of boundaries to

what was seen as the responsibility of social services contributed not only to the increase in referrals but also to the notion of social services as the scrap heap for problems – whenever there was no clear indication of what agency to approach, or a satisfactory result could not be arrived at with another department, or the problem was intractable, social services became the agency that was expected to take responsibility.

The effect of increased referral rates on social workers who were unclear and lacked confidence about their new roles, were unsure of the boundaries of responsibility of the department they worked for, and had relatively little effective backing and support (such was the confusion that reigned in many teams immediately after reorganization) was the development of what could be called a 'crisis mentality'. The high referral rates, variety of referrals, and high staff turnover coupled with few qualified and experienced staff forced many teams to concentrate on short-term crisis work, as a result of necessity rather than a professional decision about the most effective types of work. Long-term and preventive work consequently received less attention, and the lack of preventive work could be said to further increase the incidence of crisis demands – a vicious circle was in motion. One of the clear lessons arising out of Seebohm reorganization has been that social work cannot be used as a palliative in all situations of social distress, and the profession, therefore, needs to develop a clear understanding of where social work help is most likely to be effective, and concentrate work in these areas, thereby rationing agency function and social work time.

Much was confused and chaotic in the period immediately after reorganization, the effects of the mixing of staff from previously separate departments and the lack of clarity about boundaries of work being the major factors at the fieldwork level. There were also, however, positive effects from reorganization. The two major advantages appeared to be the establishment of a blueprint for area teams and the emphasis laid by the Committee on the need for research and data collection to be treated as a continuing process and a permanent feature of the new department's work. The establishment of area offices to provide easier accessibility to those in need contributed to the increase in referral rates. Dunn (1978) suggested that, whereas before 1971 many needs went unmet because of the difficulty clients found in contacting the service that they required, after the establishment of area offices and their ready accessibility the reverse is the case, and many of the requests made to area offices are not relevant to social services, who then act as an information and advisory service in referring the client to the relevant agency.

Another advantage of organization through area offices was the potential for assimilating valuable local information at a grass-roots level, which could then be fed through to central management so yielding better-informed planning decisions. Impetus was also given to acquiring local knowledge and developing co-operation with voluntary bodies to mobilize local resources. In terms of advantage to clients, apart from increased accessibility, the individual social worker practising in a generic area team had potentially more skills and more common services available to him in dealing with a range of clients, as opposed to services being exclusive to a particular client group, as had previously been the case.

The establishment of area teams

It was suggested to the Seebohm Committee that the problems posed by, and dissatisfaction felt with, the organization of the personal social services could be overcome by accommodating the staff of the different departments under one roof, whilst maintaining their membership of distinct departments. Whilst acknowledging the advisability of housing workers with related functions in one place, the Seebohm Committee opted for a much more radical alternative in the creation of large and bureaucratic social services departments with area teams as their basic fieldwork units. The establishment of area teams situated, ideally, in the geographical area which was to comprise their catchment, was seen as the most effective means of organization for the new departments. As social services departments were to be much larger organizations than their more specialized predecessors, it was suggested that their units of operation would need to be more decentralized to provide an effective service to the public. Area teams, based in area offices, were therefore seen as: the solution to problems of ensuring increased accessibility of service to potential users; facilitating closer identi-fication between social workers and the area in which they were working; providing a decentralized organization with considerable autonomy in decision making; and increasing the spirit of teamwork and mutual support amongst staff.

It was suggested that experimentation in associating area offices with other locally based services, such as health centres, primary schools, libraries, playgrounds, day nurseries, or coffee shops should be encouraged, with a view to increasing not only accessibility but also acceptability in the interests of a comprehensive approach. The Report states:

> 'We attach great importance to the comprehensive area team approach in the search for an effective family service and, as a concomitant, the delegation of the maximum authority for decisions to the area offices. The effectiveness of the service to the person or family seeking help is in the provision of prompt and skilled assistance. For this reason, we suggest that ideally each area office should be controlled by a senior professionally trained social worker with a grasp of administrative issues and wide powers of decision.'
>
> (HMSO 1968: paragraph 592)

Services, therefore, should be readily available at the point of need.

Smith and Ames (1976) suggest that the four major advantages seen to arise from organization into area teams are not necessarily achieved.

Firstly, geographical accessibility is not the only barrier to client access; factors such as acceptability, reception facilities, expectations about service, and the availability of publicity are also crucial. In many cases the subjective attitudes of clients crucially affect access to services even where there is no geographical barrier. Despite the generally increased geographical accessibility and the supposed local resource function of area teams, studies have consistently shown a lack of clarity on the part of the public about the functions of social services departments and the apparent need for more adequate publicity (e.g. Barker 1975, Sainsbury and Nixon 1979). In addition there was, and undoubtedly remains, a degree of stigma attached to approaching 'the welfare', which could be taken to be a major subjective barrier to access to service.

Secondly, they suggest that Seebohm's emphasis on the importance of social workers' links with the community/locality in which they work may have a deleterious effect on the relationship between social worker and client. Their argument is that a strategy designed to localize a professional worker may serve to distance him further from the client because, as a result of the inadequacy of resources available to the social worker, there is a desire to control the interaction between worker and client, as a defence mechanism on the part of the worker. That is, the social worker is in danger of adopting a defensive stance in response to the stress generated by clients' needs for inadequate resources.

Thirdly, in relation to the avowed importance of area teams being able to exercise considerable operational autonomy, this objective has always tended to be clouded, at times to the point of obscurity, by the heavy dependence of area teams on the powerful administrative, policy, and planning functions performed centrally – most notably in the control of resources.

Finally, the assumption that the introduction of area teams would create an environment which staff would perceive as offering them adequate professional support was challenged on the basis that, whilst organizational arrangements undoubtedly affect such factors as the amount and form of supervision, the effectiveness and freedom of communication, the sharing of responsibility, and the style of management (and are hence likely to be related to feelings of professional support), such features are not exclusive to area-team organization.

Despite such misgivings as those cited above about the advantages that accrued from area-team organization, the establishment of area teams has been hailed as one of the major benefits to have been derived from reorganization. Dunn (1978), posing the question of whether the upheaval caused by reorganization with its object of providing a better and integrated service to clients was worth it, maintains that the popular impression amongst press and public is that the changes were unsuccessful. On the other hand, Dunn himself sees as a major positive outcome the establishment of area offices facilitating both greater accessibility for potential users and the possibility of feedback from area teams, based on detailed knowledge about local needs and resources, to central management to help in planning decisions, policy making, and priority setting. A logical extension from the establishment of area teams is increased emphasis on the problems, needs, and resources of the local community. Seebohm's objective of increased interaction between the social services department (as represented by the area office) and individuals and groups in the community it is designed to serve opens the way to experimentation with social action approaches, another major and lasting benefit to accrue from reorganization. Interestingly, Liddiard (1978) notes that there are strong indications in parts of the USA that many academics and social administrators there are turning towards the idea of an integrated social service delivery system similar to that proposed by Seebohm ten years ago. As well as admiring the separation of cash assistance from the giving of direct personal services, the Americans also believe there should be an identifiable local geographical area as the basis for the delivery of personal social services. They are, therefore, working on the development of a system of local offices in highly accessible neighbourhood locations in which would be deployed social workers who were primarily generalists, with access to specialist backing.

Area teams were, therefore, established after 1971 along generally similar organizational lines, usually comprising an area officer, senior social workers, basic-grade social workers, social-work assistants, a home-help section, and administrative staff, sometimes with additional more specialized posts such as advisors for the disabled. Basic-grade social workers were supervised by a particular senior social worker, but in the early days of area teams there was often no greater structure to the teams. That is, social workers worked across the whole geographical span of their area team, and across the whole range of work of the previously specialist departments. Social workers, therefore, had to deal with the whole range of incoming work at the point of initial contact, and this work had to be subsequently allocated to an individual social worker. Senior social workers generally dealt with matters of allocation, but lines of responsibility for allocation of cases were often non-existent and depended either on good relationships between staff, or pressure on social workers to accept cases either beyond or outside their field of competence, or on which they would be unable to work effectively because of their already high case load. This lack of structure, leading to unclear lines of responsibility coupled with high case loads, increasing referrals, and low morale and confidence on the part of many staff now being expected to work generically, resulted in cases being passed from one senior to another for allocation, and hence in long waiting times from the point of initial contact to the time where the client received any service. The establishment of area teams, however, did give back to social workers a focus for their identity, albeit now on a geographical rather than distinct department-mental basis, and gradually membership of an area grew to become a leading factor in the development of a consensus about pro-fessional matters, and in the beliefs and value bases of staff. Streatfield and Mullings (1979), in a study of the communication of information in social services departments, discovered that staff interviewed found it very hard to either conceptualize or relate to the whole department, except in terms of their immediate workplace or team. The size and bureaucratic nature of the department as a whole tends to have become too remote to function as a focus for the individual worker's identity, and consequently units of the organiz-ation, in this case area teams, emerge as the most relevant and meaningful for staff membership and identity.

The Brunel study of social services departments (Social Services Organizational Research Unit 1974) describes the general function of such departments to be the prevention or relief of social distress in individuals, families, and communities, in liaison with other statu-tory and voluntary agencies. To fulfil this overall function, several tasks must be undertaken: research and evaluation, strategic planning, operational work at the community level, operational work with individuals and families, public relations, staffing and training, managerial and co-ordinative work, logistics, finance, and secretarial work. Basic-grade social workers in area teams are primarily concerned with operational work with individuals and families. This comprises the provision of basic social work services such as assessment, providing information and advice, monitoring and supervision of vulnerable individuals and families, working with individuals and families to develop or maintain their personal capacity for adequate social functioning, and arranging the pro-vision of other appropriate services. Concentration at this level means that social workers are dealing, to a very large extent, with people who may already be deemed 'social casualties', in contrast to taking a more positive preventive approach by focusing on oper-ational work at community level, which would be aimed directly at the prevention or relief of social distress at that level – for example, by assisting and supporting voluntary welfare organizations, stimu-lating the development of self-help groups, or educating the public about available services and their rights to these.

The intention of the Seebohm Committee was that the unification of the separate departments and their organization into area teams would facilitate work with individuals, families, and at a preventive community level. However, even in 1979 (eight years after re-organization) area teams were still chiefly dealing with relatively large populations and working from centralized offices. They therefore functioned largely in terms of reaction to problems presented, rather than at a primarily preventive level, problems being conceptualized primarily in individual rather than community terms. As local authority field social work tends to be conceived of as problem solving and task centred as opposed to problem preventing and system centred, it therefore responds to expressed need and can be said to be functionally apart from the community (Georgiou 1977).

Area teams can best be described as front-line organizations in that social workers, who are at the bottom of the social-services-department hierarchy, initiate work at the front line, and work flow tends to be upwards rather than downwards. Area teams, based on the ideal of decentralized decision making, therefore became the unit of organization that was faced after 1971 with structuring itself to deal with the bombardment of problems of an undifferentiated nature. The strain this in itself placed on the newly formed teams was further complicated by the lack of boundaries in the scope of work which the teams were expected to undertake, which resulted from the reorganization, the increased referral rate (estimated by Dunn (1978) to be 300 per cent), and the lack of resources (including trained and confident manpower). The increased rate of referrals and their undifferentiated nature, at a period when social workers were trying to adjust to working in large, generic departments, meant that some means had to be established to decide what work would and would not be dealt with; there had to be some system of priorities. As a result of the 'crisis mentality' of the period, the statutory duties placed with social services departments, and the search for political and public approval, highest priority was generally accorded either to those cases which required rapid and immediate action because of the high physical risk, or risk to life, as with non-accidental injury to children, suicide, and vulnerable elderly persons; or to those areas of work concerned with the courts.

That is, most work undertaken was of a crisis rather than of a preventive nature.

Area teams became the gateway through which individuals had to pass to acquire service, and the initial response of the organization to the bombardment by applicants and external referrers was to screen all referrals for their relevance to the department. In fact, in only a minority of cases (those arising out of the statutory duties of the department) does the referral have to be accepted – for example where juveniles are appearing in court, when children have to be received into care, or when compulsory admission under the Mental Health Act 1959 is required. There is, therefore, a wide degree of discretion in what is considered relevant work for the department, with different staff accepting or rejecting different sorts of referral. Hence there can easily be gross inconsistencies in the responses of those staff who are participating in this initial screening process. Furthermore, a wide range of staff may be screening referrals, ranging from receptionists and telephonists, through social workers to seniors and area officers, depending on the route of the referral. The structure of an agency, in this case the area team, can function to either promote or reduce the delivery of service – the classic examples of agency structure acting as a barrier to clients receiving a service being the generation of waiting lists. Other factors, such as the poor quality of reception facilities and lack of clear publicity, also function as barriers.

The consequence of the establishment of area teams as the gateway to service and the bombardment of such teams arising from the increased referral rate and the consequent need for teams to set priorities was that many area teams found they had to look at their own internal structure for ways to provide an effective service. Crises which arose in terms of area teams' functioning served to evoke organizational initiatives, resulting in new ways of internally structuring area teams.

2

The internal restructuring of area teams

Introduction

After reorganization and the establishment of area teams, these teams were faced with the problem of dealing with all the new incoming work for their particular geographical area. Although obviously new work had had to be dealt with in the earlier, separate departments, their client-group focus meant that the range of work and types of demands presented had a greater degree of consistency and workers built up experience and skills in particular areas of work. The new area teams were faced with a vast increase in the number and range of referrals. A motley collection of social workers from different departments, and often with mixed feelings about the organization of which they now found themselves a part, were confronted with having to provide a generic social work service to the general public. Duty-rota systems, whereby nearly all social work staff in the team took it in turn to cover duty in the office by seeing all new referrals whether by telephone or visit, and dealing with crises, proved largely unacceptable. Staff, accustomed to traditional long-term methods of work, felt little or no commitment to seeing new clients, and consequently the service clients received often amounted to little more than a note being made of their request.

It was as a result of the dissatisfaction felt with such arrangements that area teams were pushed towards examining their internal organization. This was particularly due to the concern felt for the fate of long-term work which was suffering as a result of the amount of staff time being spent in dealing with the heavy bombardment of new and crisis work. The outcome in many areas was that a model was developed whereby area teams were subdivided into intake and long-term teams.

Intake teams were, therefore, developed primarily to protect the quality of long-term work and secondly as a means of dealing more efficiently and effectively with new work to the advantage of both agency and client. However, the formation of intake teams cannot be viewed apart from the structure, function, and ethos of the whole area team and the population it serves. Consequently, matters such as the deployment of staff between teams, the brief to which different teams work, and the relationship between teams are matters for the whole area team to discuss. Where there is a lack of commitment from the area team as a whole to such a model, problems arise which threaten the successful working of that model.

The organization of incoming work after the Seebohm Report

One of the major problems confronting the newly established area teams was how to organize new incoming work in such a way that clients and referrers would receive an efficient and effective service in keeping with the spirit of the Seebohm Committee's proposals. However, the confusion that reigned after reorganization resulted in the service offered being, in many places, the very antithesis, and it was amidst this chaos that the initial impetus for the development of intake teams arose, as a pragmatic response to the existing organization.

Social workers 'at the coal face' were confronted with: an enormous increase in the demand for social work help, coupled with a shortage of resources, including manpower; an inability, due to shortage of staff, to undertake preventive work, resulting in increased crisis work; dilution and diffusion of specialist skills and knowledge, and rapid promotion of many staff, resulting in there being few experienced workers in the front line and consequently a lack of confidence among staff sometimes resulting in their adopting an aggressive/defensive stance towards those making demands upon them; and hence a general lowering of morale, professional confidence, and self-esteem on the part of staff. Lack of resources was no new problem but new legislation (the Children and Young Persons Act 1969, and the Chronically Sick and Disabled Persons Act 1970) and the Seebohm reorganization had promised much, and raised the expectations of the public and the profession, only to then cause frustration in practice. Social workers were now faced with a whole spectrum of unmet need, not just in a particular specialist field, and were hence facing an increasingly insurmountable task. In addition, with the mushrooming of social services departments other agencies were making inappropriate referrals and the pattern was established whereby social services departments often came to be viewed as the last-resort agency, the place where the buck finally stops. The increase in the number of referrals was exacerbated by the tremendously increased pressure experienced by social workers resulting from their unfamiliarity with many areas of work. Because of the much wider range of referrals to social services departments consequent upon the amalgamation of the three previously distinct departments, social workers felt under great pressure, causing high anxiety and a sense of insecurity. Contact with new clients seeking help was a positive experience for neither social worker nor client.

The majority of teams immediately after the Seebohm reorganization used duty rotas as a means of handling new incoming work. All, or nearly all, social workers in the team were on the rota, and responsible for all incoming work on the day or part-day they were on duty. Coping with duty at the best of times can be a daunting and threatening prospect, especially in view of the vast range of requests, problems, and clients with which area teams are presented. At a time when social workers had been used to practising in relatively discreet areas of work, the prospect of doing duty and coping with all comers was sufficiently threatening to become virtually immobilizing. Taking into account the fact that most social workers were used to traditional long-term models of practice, the task becomes even more daunting.

Child care officers were having to deal with the mentaly ill and compulsory admissions under the Mental Health Act 1959, of which they often had scant understanding and no experience; mental welfare officers were dealing with admissions to homes for the elderly; blind welfare officers with reception into care of children. Such a state of affairs led to the confusion of staff, other agencies, and the public alike, and resulted in such ludicrous scenes as a welfare officer used to dealing with the blind, when on duty one day and confronted by a single mother due to go into hospital and needing her three children cared for, telling the woman that she would have to go to the Children's Department; general practitioners ringing up asking for a mental welfare officer being told they were on to the wrong office; and one particularly harassed ex-welfare officer telling a client that his department only dealt with gift furniture! Seebohm's goals of an effective family service that would reach out to those in need seemed a long way off.

Such gross travesties of reorganization apart, a much more fundamental problem was the commitment, or lack of it, felt by duty officers to new referrals. Social workers were largely trained for, and experienced in, long-term casework models of practice; their case loads often consisted of very large numbers of long-term cases. Whether this was the best way of helping those clients or was an appropriate deployment of resources is a separate question; long-term casework was the order of the day. The results of research on short-term, contract, and task-centred work, although debated at a theoretical level, had yet to make its impact felt on British social work practice, especially that by local authorities. Social workers, therefore, felt their prime task was to work with their long-term clients. Consequently, having to do duty was often experienced as an unpleasant chore, and many social workers described the lack of emotional investment in clients' problems they felt when they were doing duty. They also felt they could not easily plan their own long-term work because of the intrusion of duty days and the tendency of duty work to carry over from one day to the next.

Duty officers often arranged for their own clients to call into the office on their duty days, thereby sabotaging the system to the social worker's advantage by being unavailable for duty work at these times. The result, however, was that the receptionist was left to deal with callers, and clients were either not seen or had a very long wait. When duty officers did see clients at the point of intake, they often took only the most cursory of details. This was caused by factors including lack of commitment, heightened anxiety, feelings of being bombarded, lack of knowledge or experience in the field relevant to the problem being presented, and fear of being landed with the case in the longer term. In this process the relevant features were sometimes excluded; in any event the case was then passed through, usually to the senior social worker, for allocation.

Doing duty in this way often amounted to little more than a clerical function – that is, getting some idea of what the client wants, writing this down, and passing it through the system, the duty officer then having no further responsibility. Many cases that were passed through for allocation could have been dealt with more efficiently and effectively for both social worker and client by greater staff commitment to the first interview, for a large proportion of problems presented to area teams can be adequately dealt with on the spot or else referred, after discussion, to a more appropriate agency, thereby reducing expenditure of time and resources for the agency, and reducing frustration for the client. Furthermore, under duty rota systems *ad hoc* responses are made by different duty officers, often with little sharing or consistency between different workers, resulting in inconsistent responses to clients and other referring agencies.

Duty systems as they existed in the early 1970s were, therefore, unsatisfactory in several ways. Long-term clients suffered because their social workers were too busy trying to cope with the demands of duty in the new departments in addition to their long-term case load to plan effective work with clients. First-time applicants to area teams were likely to meet a fraught, uninterested, and possibly very defensive duty officer, who would in all likelihood take down only the bare details of the problem and then say someone would be in touch; waiting lists of six to eight weeks were not uncommon. Repeated visits to the office by the client would mean contacts with a series of different duty officers, all of whom operated in very different ways and who may or may not see the particular problem as appropriate to the social services department, possibly causing even greater confusion and frustration for the client. The needs of clients at the point of referral were all too often not being met. Social workers suffering from low morale and high anxiety tended to withdraw and become defensive in response to pressure. Trained to do long-term work they were faced with an ever-increasing number and expanding variety of referrals about many of which they had little or no knowledge to fall back on.

In addition, the Seebohm reorganization had resulted in increased expectations on the part of the public – both clients and

other agencies – about the wonders the new social services departments could perform and the resources they had at their command.
Such unfulfilled expectations served to highlight the inherent contradiction of the social workers', particularly the duty officers',
position – that they are publicly trained and privately motivated to
help but must admit both to themselves and to clients that they
cannot in many instances do so, often because of inadequate
resources of all kinds. This tension between expectations and reality
can cause duty officers to take a defensive stance in response to
client's requests, which they so often had to turn down. Hence social
workers were dissatisfied with their role as duty officers, but equally
dissatisfied and disheartened with their long-term work, which they
were unable to adequately plan and develop. Such frustrations and
dissatisfactions were heightened by, and contributed to, the high
rate of staff turnover and consequent lack of qualified and experienced staff.

Area teams often harnessed their resources to ensure that clients
received some sort of service, however limited or inappropriate,
rather than setting about tackling the crucial issues of establishing
priorities and deciding what was and what was not appropriate to
social services departments and so provide an effective service to
clients. This is the familiar 'we can't help you with your feelings
about your ill health or your impossible housing conditions, but do
have a bus pass' type of intervention, and was perhaps caused by the
confusion over the role of social work by local authorities. Such a
response serves to make social workers feel they are doing something, and to assuage their guilt about the inadequacy of the
response. This type of service was often at the expense of service to
long-term clients: skilled assessment, continuing care and treatment,
review of cases, and professional decisions about closure seemed to
take second place to responding to immediate needs and crises. The
social work mentality of the time can be characterized as a crisis
mentality, and the service offered as an Elastoplast service, patching
things up in the quickest, simplest way with little concern for how
the situation arose in the first place, what other ramifications there
might be, or how this or other crises may be prevented in the future.

Finally, from an organizational point of view, the duty-rota
system was inefficient and wasteful. Low staff morale resulted in
inefficiency, duplication of effort, waste of manpower, and a heavy

burden being placed on clerical and reception staff in dealing with, and often deflecting, the incoming bombardment of work. Receptionists were often called on to make decisions and assessments over matters in which they had no experience or training, the typical example being having to rank the urgency or priority of requests, with little or no support or guidance from social work staff. Where there is a close working relationship between reception and intake staff many of these problems are relatively easily overcome and a group ethos is developed as to how requests are dealt with. Arising out of the general dissatisfactions felt by staff at the poor quality of service offered to clients, which was far from Seebohm's ideals of an effective, preventive family service reaching out to those in need in the community, there developed in many areas an impetus to look at new ways of organizing area teams internally so as to protect long-term work, and to provide speedy and effective service to new clients. That is, to seek ways of establishing a team of social workers whose remit would be to deal with all new incoming work.

The establishment of intake teams

The prime motivation in the development of intake teams was the desire to protect the quality of long-term social work, which was still seen as the proper work of the department. The Social Services Research Group, meeting in London in early 1974 to discuss the establishment of intake teams (Challis 1974), found that such teams were generally introduced to take the pressure off long-term teams by freeing them from the intrusion of duty work, thereby allowing them time to undertake planned and preventive work, and to do intensive and experimental work without the demands of short-term and crisis work, or the necessity of fulfilling information and advice functions, which were increasingly becoming a feature of the area team duty officer's role. The impetus for the establishment of intake teams can, therefore, be said to have arisen primarily out of a desire to perfect and improve established practice, rather than a desire to innovate or to develop a mode of organization more advantageous to potential applicants.

However, several advantages were seen to result from the establishment of intake teams. These were that such teams, divorced from the conflicting pressures of long-term and duty work, would provide a more complete and consistent service to clients, with duty and short-term work becoming the field to which the social workers in such teams had a positive commitment, rather than tolerated by virtue or lack of choice and experienced as disruptive to the mainstream work. Social workers in intake teams were expected to develop the knowledge and skills to provide a good assessment and short-term service to clients; accurate assessment being followed by immediate response rather than the protracted waiting period often experienced by clients before, now that intake workers no longer had to cope with the demands of a long-term case load.

The establishment of a group of workers dealing with all new referrals within the area, whether by letter, phone, or visit, was seen as a way of building links with other agencies and improving liaison between them and social services, in contrast to the frustration often voiced by other agencies when confronted by a series of (often anonymous) duty officers, each with their own ideas about what did and did not constitute an appropriate case for the social services department. Such improved links between intake teams and other agencies in the area not only facilitated the referral process but, by intake members giving a more consistent response than was often the case previously, served a two-way educative function by informing both agencies about their own and the other's role, organization, and style of work. Clients would thereby benefit from more informed advice, and referrals to other agencies – or from these agencies to the area team – were more likely to be appropriate.

Finally, the establishment of intake teams gave increased impetus to the original Seebohm goal of improved data collection to inform service planning. There was now both a focus to and purpose for the collection and collation of data about incoming work – what sort of work was being referred, by whom, how (leter, telephone, visit, etc.), and what was the outcome. With intake teams providing a more consistent service to clients such data were easily available and more consistently codified than when there was a series of individual and *ad hoc* responses. However, the problem of classification of problems and their standardization for statistical purposes continues to pose major problems, often even within one team, and increasing inconsistencies tend to arise between different areas, even when they are ostensibly working to the same brief within one borough. The calculation of re-referral rates and the classification of cases are particular areas of frequent disagreement; for example, deciding whether a mildly handicapped elderly person is classified as an elderly person or a physically handicapped person depends on some view about the nature of the ageing process and whether or not a degree of handicap is a 'normal' concomitant. Consequently, the validity of the cross-comparability of statistics between different area teams in one borough is questionable, and between boroughs virtually impossible.

The establishment of intake teams was, therefore, expected to benefit long-term clients by freeing social workers to work more intensely and innovatively with these groups, and to benefit new and short-term clients by dealing with them more quickly, consistently, efficiently, and effectively than had been the case. From the point of view of the agency it would offer an improved form of organization to cope with the (usually increasing) volume of referrals; would be more economic in the use of social work time; and more able to cope with fluctuating demand, such as periods of rapid increase in the referral rate. Also, the establishment of an intake team was expected to systematize procedures at intake, and facilitate accurate recording of all contacts made. Improved data collection could be used both in planning and policy development by central management and by the area team as a means of demonstrating their demands for new and expanded resources with hard information about need.

After the decision to consider setting up an intake team – a team of workers, including administrative and clerical staff, committed to dealing with new and short-term work – the next debate tended to be on what kind of staff were required in such a team. Young-husband (1978a) commented that many people calling at an area office wanted information or advice, or to make a straightforward service request, such as for a home help, meals on wheels, welfare aids, or residential accommodation for the elderly. Although such requests may properly be the province of the social services department, she questioned whether they could not be more properly dealt with by non-professional staff, always assuming that adequate consultation and back-up was available. Many departments have built-in filters for certain types of request; for example, requests for a home help often go direct to the home-help organizer, and requests for aids direct to the advisor for the disabled, both of whom are usually closely related to area-team social workers and refer back if problems of a more complex nature than the original request suggested are found.

However, as discussed in the previous section, when dealing with the filtering aspect of the intake process someone has to initially ascertain what the request is for and this process in itself can become a complex one, full of pitfalls for both the applicant (who may either not know what services are available, what exactly they want, or be unable to clearly articulate their need) and for agency staff, for the initial stated request may be much more complex than it first appears. Without wanting to suggest that social work should return to the time when the traditional criticism was that whatever the client presented as the problem (even if it were a straightforward request for a service) the social worker always looked for an underlying problem (often at the expense of dealing with the client's initial request), it can be suggested that in reaction to this the pendulum has swung to the other extreme and the current tendency is for only the presenting problem to be considered. This will be discussed further in Chapter 4. It is sufficient to say here that suggestions that unqualified staff should perhaps be those to deal with the initial intake process seem to negate many of the advantages supposed to accrue from the establishment of generic teams, and many of the potential advantages of the establishment of intake teams in relation to providing a thorough assessment with preventive potential. Gill and Boaden (1976), in an article advocating that intake work demands particular skills and experience on the part of social workers, comment that they see the greatest danger in the setting up of intake teams being the belief that such work is very similar to reception and simply a matter of common sense.

In addition, and in response particularly to the traditional emphasis on long-term casework as the 'heart' of the work – that which is accorded high status – there was, and perhaps remains, a danger that intake work would be seen as a sort of weeding out process, dealing with the dull and routine cases and leaving the exciting, complex cases for long-term workers; intake would be no more than a clearing ground for long-term social work. The direct offshoot of such thinking is that the less experienced, less qualified staff are those that work in intake teams, reserving the 'real' work for the highly qualified, experienced social workers of the long-term teams. Such fears were often alluded to in the literature on the setting up of intake teams in the first half of the 1970s, and must be related to the dominance of long-term casework theory taught on social work courses at the time, and consequently the perception of this as the essence of social work. With an increasing amount of literature on short-term, task-centred, contract, and crisis work, and the emergence of the unitary approach, the anxieties have now shifted and in discussion of intake-team organization in the latter part of the 1970s one of the fears often expressed is that long-term teams will be left with all the difficult, intractable cases, while intake teams will deal with the more interesting, rewarding, and potentially effective short-term and crisis work.

The British Association of Social Workers' paper on the Social Work Task (British Association of Social Workers 1977) concentrates on the vexed issue of specialization in social work and proposed a tripartite division of labour; newly qualified social workers to work as generalists, although they may have some special interest; social work specialists with post-qualification training to work with certain client groups or types of intervention, either face-to-face with clients, or in planning and policy development; and experienced general-purpose social workers with a wide knowledge of how to help with a range of problems, linked with assessment skills on referral to more specialist workers or agencies. The paper envisaged that much intake and short-term work would be undertaken by such practitioners – experienced, general-purpose social workers, who would become specialists in this area of work. In the Brunel study of social services departments, one ex-child care officer is quoted as commenting:

'The best control mechanism for intake is a highly skilled intake officer with particular personality and assessment skills that are different from those for long-term caseworkers. Administrative skills, ability to organize several concurrent tasks, an ability to cope with anxiety, and strong supportive control from a senior are the necessary ingredients for intake assessment.'
                    (Social Services Organizational Research Unit 1974: 181)

Similarly, Neill *et al.*, in a study of the views and attitudes of social workers in Southampton in June 1972 (after the department had been integrated for three months), concluded: 'It is clear from this study as well as from other developments in social services in many

parts of the country that one specialism of the future which cuts
right across the old divisions will be intake, assessment, and short-
term intervention' (Neill 1973: 461). Hence it seems clear that one of
the major requirements of an intake team, contributing to its success
for both the agency and the service offered to clients, is that it should
contain a good proportion of qualified and experienced staff, for the
task of the team is much more complex than an extended reception
service, and requires of the social worker a wide range of knowledge
and skills. It may be that the intake social worker is the sort of
generic social worker envisaged by the Seebohm Committee; that is,
a worker able to deal competently with a wide range of problems,
given the availability of adequate support and specialist consultant
facilities.

The rationale behind the setting up of intake teams was that
organizational rearrangement would lead to a more efficient way of
meeting expressed need, and that information about unmet need
would be more easily available to an intake team than to the more *ad
hoc* system of duty-rota organization, and could be more rationally
conveyed to the policy makers and planners within the department.
As Georgiou says: 'Intake teams evolved as a more adequate coping
mechanism to match needs and resources. It was innovated,
pioneered and used by social workers as an internal rationalization
of an area team to meet an essentially external pressure of demands'
(Georgiou 1977: 62).

The increase in resources resulting from the establishment of an
intake team is primarily an increase in staff output. That is, the
development of intake teams was a pragmatic, organizational
response to the establishment of unified social services departments
based at fieldwork level in area teams, rather than a professional
response in terms of social work theory. However, this pragmatic,
organizational response has tended to be perpetuated as a professional tool, and indeed there are sound social work reasons for
this. The professional merits of the development of intake teams are
that: it allows some workers to concentrate on developing their skills
in long-term work; it establishes a mechanism to respond quickly
and honestly to expressed need; it gives a broad overview of the
needs being brought to the department and, therefore, potentially
allows for better matching of needs and resources and more
informed priority setting; the pooling of resources and sharing of

experience, knowledge, and information in an intake team benefits both clients and staff; and the concentration of requests through a single channel, not just through one door but through a specific group of workers established for the purpose of dealing with new applicants, allows for a more rational use of resources and gives rise to potential for assessing how the service functions.

The last point is of particular relevance in considering the rate of re-referrals, which can be viewed as a crude measure of how effectively the team is meeting need. There are, however, various interpretations that can be put on re-referral rates; for example, does a high rate of re-referrals mean that needs are not being met or that clients are so satisfied with the service received they return over other matters? Re-referral rates are fascinating for speculation but caution is required before jumping to any conclusions. In administrative terms an intake structure facilitates better planned social work intervention in relation to available resources than when work was done and decisions taken on an individual, *ad hoc* basis. It gives a truer picture of demand as all referrals are coming through one channel; it maximizes the knowledge and information available by concentrating the manpower resources of the agency concerned with a specific area of work into one team; intake workers are likely to try to deal with a case at the point of referral, thereby encouraging a faster flow of work and more efficient use of staff time, rather than the duplication of effort often found in other systems. Also, periods of acute demand can be handled by a separate intake team without threatening long-term work.

The task of the intake worker is to ascertain what the client sees as the problem, explore this with him, assess his strengths and weaknesses, establish what methods he has already tried to deal with the problem, and then to recommend a course of action and facilitate its being taken. This catalogue of tasks is relevant to virtually all clients likely to present themselves to an intake worker, from individuals seeking help with housing problems or advice about financial difficulties, to families seeking help in coping with a mentally ill member and single parents requesting that their children be received into care.

Owing to the organizational changes central to the establishment of intake teams, many teams experienced an increase in staff morale after these changes. The intake worker on duty, now relieved of his long-term case load, felt less harassed, although in all likelihood had to deal with a greater proportion of new incoming work. Consequently, more time was spent at the initial interview stage and the initial assessment was likely to be much fuller. A worker who is committed to intake and sees work with new clients as his prime responsibility is likely to give a much more positive response to new clients. In addition, as Loewenstein (1974) pointed out, the duty system militated against the accumulation and consolidation of knowledge about problems, policies, and procedures, whereas intake-team members rapidly build up and consolidate such knowledge to the advantage of clients, who get better informed advice, and to workers, who are more confident about their role and more committed to it. Likewise the increased liaison with other agencies facilitates increased understanding and co-operation.

The potential advantages of intake-team organization are, therefore: increased staff morale with commitment to the task in hand; better assessment work at the initial interview, coupled with greater clarity about the role of the worker and agency; increased knowledge of, and communication with, outside agencies; greater consistency in response to clients; improved matching of needs and resources; and speedier response to expressed need. Given these potential advantages and the increasing number of individuals who use the one door of the social services department as their first port of call with a problem, query, or request for service, intake is in a position to function in a preventive manner both in terms of developing an early awareness of newly emergent needs, and in relation to dealing with individual or family problems at a time when there is a reasonable chance of preventing breakdown. Hence it can be argued that intake teams as front-line organizations are well situated to work preventively at both the community and individual/family levels. Whether or not this potential is realized will be discussed in Chapter 4.

The structure and composition of intake teams

Having established that all areas must have some sort of intake process to deal with the inflow of work and that intake teams were developed as a means of coping more efficiently and effectively with this work to the advantage of both agency and client, it is of considerable significance to examine the factors that need to be taken into account in considering the structure and composition of the proposed team. Loewenstein defined intake as 'the process and procedure which take place from the initial contact of a client with a social services department, whether this be by telephone, letter or personal contact, including the assessment of the problem, to the allocation of the case to a social worker' (Loewenstein 1974: 116). That is, the process of intake has various facets, including both clerical/administrative and social work functions. Denham narrows this down and adopts a pragmatic definition of an intake team as:

> 'the allocation of two or more individuals to cover most or all of an area team's intake work. Typically, the intake team will be expected to perform office duty as well as receive new referrals by letter and telephone, it will form initial assessments, and have a remit to provide a short-term service (6–12 weeks) where appropriate to as many new clients as possible.'
>
> (Denham 1976: ii)

The implication, although it is not actually stated, is that the 'individuals' are social workers. Corrie makes this explicit: 'By "intake group" is meant a special group of social workers responsible for all initial contact with and assessment of clients who contact the social services department, whether by telephone, letter, in person or in another agency/person' (Corrie 1976: 713). This definition seems the clearest and most comprehensive but ignores the crucial role of reception staff – including the switchboard operator for telephone referrals – in mediating clients' initial contacts with the department, and who, although they usually work for the whole area team, seem functionally closest to the intake team and form a part of it.

Other staff members may also be most logically located in the intake team; for example, the advisor for the disabled, most of whose work is of an assessment and advisory nature, and who can advise social work staff about the many requests for aids for the handicapped that are presented at intake. Hence there are staff other than social workers who may also be considered as members of the intake team depending on the structure of the department and area team. Reception and switchboard staff play such a major role in relation to the initial contact the client has with the agency, often giving advice or a sympathetic ear to waiting clients, that their work seems inextricably interwoven with that of the intake team, and their membership of that team helps them to see and understand some of the difficulties facing social workers, and to feel more confident and better supported in terms of fulfilling their own role.

When considering setting up an intake team, careful thought needs to be given to its structure and membership. Initially, therefore, a clear picture is required of the area to be served. Most teams have available to them some facts and figures on the number of referrals the team receives, what types of cases they are, how they are referred, etc. If such information is either not available or inadequate it is advisable to attempt to set up a pilot study over a short period to accumulate information about these factors. The most important are probably information about the number of new referrals per week or month; the types of case; whether they are self-referrals or referred by a friend, acquaintance, or outside agency; and whether the referral route is by a visit to the office, a telephone call, or a letter. The outcome of such referrals and the waiting time before allocation also needs to be taken into account, as does the existing work load of the whole area team. Types of referrals and the composition of the population to be served by the intake team, taken together with the siting of the area office, suggest whether the main bombardment is likely to be by telephone or personal callers to the office, or perhaps referrals from another agency.

Take, for example, an area with a high proportion of elderly and physically handicapped in the population, who are concentrated in an area of relatively poor housing stock some distance from the area office. It is unlikely that many of these clients will be able to get to the area office and, therefore, many referrals can be expected by telephone and letter. In addition if there was a voluntary organization working with the elderly in that area, the intake team may well receive many referrals via this outside agency. Contrastingly, an area team located on a large council housing estate consisting primarily of two- and three-bedroom properties is likely to deal with a high proportion of family problems and because of the location of the office and the general mobility of the population served, it is highly likely that most referrals would be by means of personal visits to the office.

Considerations such as these play a major part in planning the structure of an intake team and the type of intake process. The establishment of an intake team creates a group likely to be particularly interested in and affected by such practical matters as waiting room and interviewing facilities and the internal layout of the offices, because such factors affect primarily the ease, comfort, and general atmosphere within which the intake worker functions and within which the client is received.

In the first geographical area described above it is likely that intake workers will have to do a fair amount of home visiting, as many clients will not be able to get to the office, hence working to an office appointment system would not be appropriate, at least for that group of elderly handicapped clients, and alternative means of contact would have to be used. In the second area described, it could be assumed that a large number of families with children would be likely to call at the office, thus highlighting the need for a play area with toys in the waiting area, and perhaps someone available to keep an eye on the children while the parent is interviewed. Even from this simple comparison it is clear how the composition of different areas places differing requirements on the structure and composition of an intake team.

Hall *et al.* (1976) studied patterns of telephone bombardment of social services departments and found that up to 25 per cent of calls were direct from clients, and a large number of these were requesting advice and information. They suggest that an impersonal telephone call to the agency may seem less threatening to the client than a personal visit. The telephone intake arrangements encountered in the study supported the stereotype of the local authority as a faceless, impersonal bureaucracy. Social workers on duty did not give their names or, worse, announced: 'This is the duty officer'. The caller was not asked if they were calling from a pay-phone or where they were, and there was no offer by the social workers to call back when the money ran out. Consequently, if most referrals are likely to come to the intake team by telephone, careful consideration needs to be paid to how such calls are received. The switchboard operator plays a major role, especially if the intake worker is not immediately available, and can overcome the faceless bureaucracy stereotype by taking the caller's number and asking the social worker to ring when free, or taking down basic details so that the social worker can deal with the matter when available. Such principles obviously apply to all callers and not only to intake clients, but where the switchboard operator and receptionist feel themselves to be part of a team they are more likely to conform to the norms of that group, which are hopefully geared towards good practice.

Having studied the number, route, and nature of referrals coming in to the area team, along with information about the existing work load of the area team, the structure and composition of the intake team can be decided upon. It is very important for the whole area team to be included in such discussion, not just potential intake-team members, as the setting up of an intake team has implications for the whole area team, and to a lesser extent for the whole department.

Although not always the case when intake teams were first established in the early 1970s, most intake teams today expect to have their own senior social worker. The intake senior can then be readily available to team members to offer guidance and to take part in informal case discussions and help in decision making. Such a structure also serves to free long-term seniors from responsibility for supervising duty work, and so enables them to better plan and organize supervision and allocation within their own team and be available to give support to their own social workers. No one senior social worker can be expected to be duty senior every day, so there needs to be a degree of flexibility and co-operation between seniors so that the intake senior can occasionally get out of the office to attend, for example, departmental meetings and case conferences and have time free to supervise intake workers. On the whole, however, intake workers appreciate having a senior social worker who understands and is closely in contact with the day-to-day working of the intake team, and who knows the pressures on and priorities of the team and the strengths and weaknesses of individual workers. With such a senior, matters such as allocation, priorities, and decisions as to what is and is not appropriate for the intake team to deal with are approached with shared communication and common objectives between all members of the team.

Intake teams also find it useful to have their own senior to act on their behalf when it comes to relating to long-term teams, especially where there is potential conflict. Intake teams apparently now normally have their own seniors, and this is probably related to the

increased size of many intake teams over the past decade. Loewenstein (1974) describes an intake team in 1974 with two members and
Rapp (1974) discusses a one-man intake system in the same year.
Contrastingly, three years later Goldberg *et al.* (1977) describe an
intake team of one senior social worker, five full-time and one
part-time social workers, and a part-time advisor for the disabled to
serve a population of 73,000; in 1979 there were intake teams
comprising two seniors, seven social workers, three social work
assistants, and a part-time advisor for the disabled for a population
of 55,000. Whilst it is clearly not practical to have a senior social
worker for just one or two social workers, with a trend towards
larger intake teams it seems a natural development that intake
teams should have their own seniors.

The size and composition of the team obviously depends on the
number and type of referrals coming in. To return again to the
example of the area with a high proportion of elderly and physically
handicapped in the population – accepting the reality that at present
much work with the elderly and the handicapped is done on a
service delivery basis by social work assistants – it is reasonable to
suggest that an intake team serving this kind of area would be well
advised to include one or more social work assistants among their
number. Contrastingly, the second area, with a high concentration
of young families, may require a lower proportion of social work
assistants in the intake team and more qualified social workers,
perhaps including one with an extensive knowledge of welfare rights.

In addition to considering social work staff in the intake team,
attention also needs to be paid to the administrative and clerical
staff and their commitment because for an intake-team system, with
its relatively high turnover of cases, to function effectively it is vital
that the administrative system works efficiently so that files can be
quickly traced and information retrieved. This requires a reasonable
degree of commitment to intake by administrative and clerical team
members.

Corrie (1976), in a survey of the 32 London boroughs carried out
in 1973–4, discovered that 16 boroughs had intake teams in some of
their areas, resulting in 27 area teams having intake teams. These
teams were sent questionnaires covering several topics, one of which
was designed to ascertain the proportion of the total social workers
in the area team who were in the intake team. There was a general

belief that a large proportion of incoming cases could be dealt with on a short-term basis, and obviously the amount of work of this sort a team sees itself as handling to a great extent determines the proportion of social workers in the team. Replies varied, between 15 per cent and 50 per cent of the total area-team social workers being in the intake team, the average being 37.5 per cent.

As well as depending on the number and type of referrals and the proportion of incoming work that is expected to be dealt with on a one-off or short-term basis, the size and structure of an intake team also depends on the structure and composition of the long-term teams in the area office (including their ability to take up new long-term cases quickly), and on the existence of other agencies in the area, their proximity to the area office, and their accessibility to clients. For example, if the local Family Service Unit is committed to short-term family therapy, then a number of referrals that may otherwise have been dealt with by an intake social worker may be referred to the Family Service Unit. Similarly if there is a Citizens Advice Bureau very close to the area office the intake team may refer to them clients coming in with problems about fuel-supply dis-connections and Supplementary Benefit Appeal Tribunals, whereas if no such agency existed locally, or if the intake worker knew it was often closed due to pressure of work, or if clients had to wait a long time to be seen and there were no facilities for children, then the intake worker might deal with the case personally.

A further consideration in establishing an intake team is the personal skills and preferences of workers. Both the type and pace of work is quite different in intake to in long-term work, and some individuals will feel better suited to one type of work than to others. The personal preferences of workers are of considerable importance, as obviously the likely success of an intake team is increased by including workers who feel a commitment to, and are comfortable with, this style of work. Corrie (1976), in her survey, questioned whether personality factors were seen as important in the selection of intake-team members; twenty-five respondents replied yes, three no, and three that they did not know. Only five respondents had had any special training before forming their intake team.

Some departments, presumably because they were aware of the differences between intake and long-term work, the importance of workers feeling committed to team objectives, and the stress under which intake workers function which affects each individual differently, built in provisions to allow social workers to change teams after certain periods. Such changes are really only organizationally expedient if they occur at times of other staff turnover in the area, because too much movement between intake and long-term teams could have divisive effects on both teams and militate against establishing a stable group cohesion. The advantages to staff in both teams of having experience and understanding of each other's work, with consequent potential cross-fertilizations of skills and knowledge – so that, for example, long-term team members may use more short-term, task-centred methods in their work – have to be set against the disruption caused (particularly to long-term clients) if their social worker changes every few months, and to the individual and the rest of the team in intake, where the high degree of group cohesion often means a series of adjustments are necessary to incorporate a new member. When an area team is setting up a new organizational structure comprising intake and long-term teams, ideally experienced staff should be divided between the teams.

Experienced workers are vital to intake to provide an efficient service with quick and accurate assessment work, to be able to take decisions, deal with crises, and work under stress. But experienced workers are also necessary for long-term teams, to protect the quality of long-term work, and by having the confidence and skill to innovate, and the experience to take over complex long-term cases from intake workers. Corrie found that on balance the London Borough area teams tended to concentrate their experienced workers in intake. It would certainly seem to be the case, from the experience of various intake teams, that where an intake team consists largely of unqualified or inexperienced staff, they are less able to stand up under strain and may collapse at points of crisis, for example during acute staff shortages, on loss of an intake senior, or during a rapid increase in the number of referrals. Qualified and experienced teams subject to the same strains, although suffering as a result and having to devise some strategy to cope, seem better able to survive. Problems such as staff shortages, lack of resources, and long periods of coping with empty posts seem all too characteristic of social services departments and hence it seems advisable, whilst still working to overcome some of these obstacles, to accept their reality and plan so that such fluctuations have a minimum effect. Having a relatively high proportion of qualified and experienced staff in intake therefore makes sense because it is this team that bears the brunt of the area's work load, and where it is much more difficult to protect staff from the demands made by clients.

Allocation of work between and within teams

Intake teams are not generally geographically based – that is they cover the whole geographical span of the area team – whereas long-term teams can be organized in a number of ways. They are often organized on a patch basis, each long-term team being responsible for the long-term work in a particular geographical sub-area of the area team. Alternatively some areas organize their long-term teams along specialist lines, reminiscent of the pre-Seebohm era, having different long-term teams dealing with under fives, adolescents, the mentally ill, the elderly, etc. In some areas long-term teams have no particular focus, either client group or geographical patch, but are linked only by being supervised by a particular senior.

Where long-term teams are organized on a geographical patch basis, if it is agreed that an intake case should be transferred to a long-term worker then it is quite clear to which long-term team the case belongs: the one which covers the client's home address. With the second option there is a grave danger, currently being experienced by some areas which operate this system, of arguments similar to those characteristic of the pre-Seebohm era – for example, over whether the children who are under five, mother's mental illness, or 84-year-old granny's state of health and disability is the real problem. The result of such disputes is that the responsibility for accepting a case for long-term allocation is far from clear at times and leads to bargaining between long-term seniors on the basis of such factors as the staffing levels in their teams, and how pressured each team feels. The danger of such a system for intake is that the intake worker is left holding the case while the bargaining is sorted out. With increasing moves towards specialisms in social services departments, these problems may be on the increase as more specialist teams are developed.

The same difficulties arise, probably even more so, where an intake team deals with a number of long-term teams each headed by a senior but with no other distinguishing characteristics. Again, long-term allocation becomes a matter of bargaining between long-term seniors. Although most intake teams undertake short-term work, some deal only with duty and assessment work and then pass the case on for allocation. This means that either long-term teams also undertake short-term work, or that as well as intake and long-term teams there may be a team with a remit to undertake short-term work. The apparent advantages of this latter model are that there would need to be only a small number of social workers in intake as their brief would be limited, and there would be developed in the short-term team a high level of expertise in this type of work. Set against these are the difficulties in many cases of separating assessment and short-term work and the problem for the client of having to change worker if short-term work was planned, and possibly again if the case became long-term. Such a model seems cumbersome and open to transfer blocks at two points. The apparent advantages of the model are easily incorporated by having a larger intake team with the capacity to do short-term work and thereby become experienced in such work. This last form of organization is also more likely to give workers more job satisfaction than the previous model, where intake workers would have little chance of seeing any of their work through to its conclusion.

A model which tries to incorporate the best of both patch and intake organization comprises what can only be described as a 'hybrid' of intake-based and patch-based systems. Social workers are organized into patch-based teams, each of which has their own senior, but then each patch team nominates (for example) two of its workers as 'duty workers'. If, therefore, there are three patch-based teams, each nominating two duty workers, this gives a duty team of six social workers, each ideally dealing only with referrals that come in from their own patch. The role of the senior social worker, if there is a senior for the duty team, becomes complex. The duty senior in theory has responsibility for supervising day-to-day duty matters and for organizing the duty team to deal with new incoming work. The duty social workers are, therefore, responsible to two seniors, the duty senior for duty matters that need to be dealt with on the spot, and their patch senior for other matters. All incoming cases that need to be allocated are passed through to the patch senior to be dealt with by their team.

Whilst such a system overcomes some of the problems claimed to result from the intake/long-term division – for example, long-term teams do get a better overview of all the work coming into their patch in this model – there are obvious difficulties in relation to duty workers being responsible to two seniors, leaving the door wide open to manipulation and games playing should the social workers feel so inclined. Also, the flexibility of the system is reduced if duty workers deal only with cases from their own patch, for there are likely to be times when there are two crises and three other people waiting to be seen from one patch, and nothing going on in the other two. Although the duty workers from these other patches are likely to help out at such times, this negates much of the benefit seen to accrue from this model – that each patch deals with all its incoming work. In addition, because the duty worker is also a member of a patch team, this may result in pressure being put on the duty worker to take on some long-term cases which cannot otherwise be allocated within the patch team. The duty worker is then placed under the conflicting pressures of dealing with intake and long-term work, resulting in many of the problems experienced under the duty-rota systems, to which intake teams were seen as the answer.

As well as allocation of work between teams, primarily between intake and long-term, there is also the question of allocation of work within the intake team for those cases that need follow-up, further assessment, or are taken on for task-centred or contract work. Where possible, direct allocation to the social worker who has done the initial interview seems favoured, in that it serves to encourage the social worker to deal fully with clients that come in and to carefully consider their plans, knowing they are likely to have to follow them through, and it saves the client from confusing changes of worker. However, such direct allocation is not always possible – for example, the duty intake worker may have dealt with several cases on that day that all need further work and his or her existing work load may be such that they cannot take on any more, or perhaps another intake worker has a particular interest in and experience of the particular type of problem being presented. Cases dealt with by intake workers therefore often need reallocation within the intake team. In relation to this a specific senior for the intake team again fulfils a useful function, as one who knows how individuals within the team are placed to take on extra work, and what can and cannot reasonably be expected of them. Some teams deal with these issues of allocation by the intake senior looking at all the cases that need allocating and then discussing with individual team members what work they are able to take on. Other teams meet at regular intervals, some as often as daily, others weekly or fortnightly, and all referrals needing allocation within the team will be discussed and a group decision made as to who should deal with what. Some cases may be felt to be more appropriately dealt with by passing them straight through for a long-term team to deal with.

The organization of area teams into long-term and intake teams requires that certain categories of work are looked at and decisions taken about how they are to be dealt with, in terms both of the organizational interests of the area team and of the individual interests of social workers. Many areas found when they established intake teams that intake workers wanted to retain one or two long-term cases. The expectation generally was that intake workers would carry very few, if any, long-term cases, because if they were subject to too much pressure from long-term work they would once more be faced with the conflicting demands of intake and long-term work. Corrie (1976) found that in twenty-five of the twenty-seven intake teams she surveyed social workers could carry long-term cases; in thirteen teams this was between one and five cases, and in nine teams ten to twenty cases. This latter figure would seem too high to be realistic if the social worker was expected to do effective long-term work as well as function as a fully integrated member of an intake team, and may be accounted for partly in terms of the time at which Corrie carried out the survey, that is 1973–74, when intake teams were often still in their infancy and the pre-Seebohm heritage of huge case loads was still being whittled down. Today an intake worker carrying much more than five long-term cases of any weight would be hard pushed to function in a fully fledged intake team.

Some area teams classify certain types of work as either the responsibility of intake or long-term teams, for example fostering applications, Guardian *ad litem* and adoption enquiries, court work, and Part III assessments. How such decisions are made depends largely on the structure of the area team and of the whole department – for example, the role of specialists in the team and department, whether there is a central fostering and adoption section, and whether the long-term teams are sufficiently well staffed to have the capacity to react speedily to requests for court reports.

How responsibility for these areas of work is sorted out is not highly important, as long as there is some clear and generally understood ruling so that which team takes responsibility is not decided solely according to some sort of *ad hoc* lottery. Any such ruling also needs to incorporate a fair degree of flexibility so that social workers in different teams have some opportunity to gain a variety of experience; for example, there is no inherent reason why an intake worker should not undertake some foster-parent assessments as long as their work load permits and other intake members agree. Likewise, there is no reason why a long-term worker should not undertake some short-term work if their work load permits and they would like to gain this experience.

Where problems tend to arise in intake is when members want to undertake work in an area that takes a substantial commitment of time, thereby reducing their availability for intake work, including the time actually spent on duty. The obvious example of such an area of work is inclusion in intermediate treatment programmes. Even this is not necessarily impossible but depends on the staffing levels and work load of the team and needs to be discussed amongst the whole intake team and taken as a shared decision so that other team members are aware of and agree to the fact that the member will have less capacity to take on short-term and duty work for a given period, otherwise there is a danger of growing resentment resulting in a lack of co-operation.

In conclusion, in establishing an intake team clarity and simplicity of organization emerge as key features, coupled with flexibility and the need for free communication both within and between teams. All area-team members need to be clear about what types of cases are expected to be dealt with by intake and what by long-term; about how short-term cases are defined; about how the transfer between intake and long-term is to be effected when necessary; and about who makes decisions and how areas of responsibility are defined. The organization of duty cover within the intake team needs to be clearly laid out so that intake members know what is expected of them. The simpler the model, the more chance it stands of success.

As an example of the problems created when certain fundamental issues are not clarified Denham (1976), in discussion of what different teams decided on as a working definition of 'short-term', found that most teams she studied, ten out of fifteen, used 'short-term' to describe cases assessed as needing 6–12 weeks' work. Two areas, however, rejected this as too simplistic and tried to formulate a definition in terms of case complexity and extent of social work involvement, on the grounds that this was more meaningful. However, at the time of the study both teams were experiencing practical difficulties with their definitions, resulting in uncertainty on the part of intake workers about when and whether to transfer cases. Even given the wide variety of variables that can be considered in trying to evaluate the success of intake teams, twenty-six out of thirty-two responses (over 80 per cent) in Corrie's study saw the intake system as 'successful'. These variables include stability of the intake group, the effectiveness of the service given, the speed with which cases are handled, and the rate of re-referrals – and the debates that surround each.

3

Considerations for efficient and effective organization of intake teams

Introduction

As a result of intake teams being established with a remit to deal with all new referrals, to deal with crises on cases not known to other social workers, and – in most cases – to take on short-term work, there developed an increased commitment to provide a positive service for new clients, rather than a message-taking service, as had often been the case in duty rota systems. In addition to the greater consideration awarded to the intake service given by social workers, the existence of a team dealing exclusively with new and short-term referrals – and thereby inextricably interwoven with the reception services – also serves to highlight the importance of the quality of reception and the impact of initial contacts on the client's subsequent dealings with the department.

For an intake team to function effectively, therefore, it needs to develop a close working relationship with reception staff to offer the best service to the client. As a result of the unpredictable level of bombardment, the anxiety generated by constantly dealing with new cases (whether in crisis or not), and the vast diversity of demands and expectations placed upon intake workers, the support and security they derive from colleagues is at a premium, and the group cohesion of functioning intake teams is generally found to be high. It has been suggested that insufficient importance is attached by some social work managers to the selection of team members, and that the appointment of a good social worker but unsuitable team member is likely to threaten the team cohesion and support. For intake teams to survive and maintain the flexibility to absorb a variety of demands, there has to be an agreed process for disposing of cases, otherwise a bottleneck occurs in the model – for if intake continues to take on new work but cannot transfer work of a long-term nature, the system clogs and eventually breaks down when the intake team becomes saturated and cannot take on any more.

Consequently a major consideration for the effective working of an intake team is its relationship with the long-term teams in the area. Problems of transferring cases between intake and long-term teams are to a degree inherent in an intake/long-term model, but need not become dysfunctional or insurmountable where relationships between the teams are open, and problems of élitism are overcome.

Components of the intake process

The intake process theoretically incorporates a number of different functions.

FILTERING

Firstly, and fundamentally, the intake process acts as a filtering process. Applicants arrive at the area office with a problem, request, or demand, and the first matter to establish is whether the social services department is the appropriate agency to deal with the applicant. This may appear a relatively straightforward task, but is not so in practice, particularly as social services departments tend to be increasingly viewed as information and advice centres in their own right. This initial filtering is often undertaken by clerical/reception staff. Take the following, apparently straightforward, presentations to an area team and the possible immediate filtering that takes place: 'I've come about my pension' – referred to the Department of Health and Social Security; 'The landlord is tipping rubbish in my garden' – advised to see the tenancy relations officer; 'My mother is ill' – referred back to the family doctor as a medical problem. All three problems seem at first glance reasonably clear statements that are properly the province of another agency and should be referred to that agency. But reality is, as ever, more complex, and a fuller discussion may prove that the problem is more complex, and appropriately the concern of the social services department.

For example, in the first case, the pensioner has received an electricity bill, is unable to pay it, and someone has told her about heating allowances. She has queried it with the DHSS visiting officer who says she is already getting a heating allowance. The pensioner argues that it is not enough and her husband, who is bronchitic, will die if the electricity supply is disconnected. She is advised to appeal to the Supplementary Benefits Tribunal, but does not know how to go about this or what it entails. In the second case, not only is the landlord tipping rubbish in the garden, but the tenant is a single parent with a physically handicapped child. They live in an upstairs flat, the accommodation is inadequate, the child cannot get downstairs alone, they are behind with the rent, and the relationship with the landlord is worsening. In the third case the caller's mother is in her eighties and ill, the doctor says there is nothing he can do, and the consultant geriatrician has visited but is not prepared to admit the old lady to hospital. Although a medical problem at source, it has implications for the daughter and her family in terms of travelling to and fro visiting, cooking, cleaning, and trying to get the old lady to her outside toilet, all of which combine to place excessive strain on the daughter, who herself suffers from a heart complaint. Thus what seems a comparatively simple question of filtering requests to a more appropriate agency can be a more complex matter, including elements that can be viewed as very much the province of the social services department.

Premature filtering, therefore, without a fairly full discussion of the relevant matters, can deprive applicants of the service they require. The situation is further complicated by the fact that there is very little, in terms of types of request for help, that social services departments cannot reject, if they so choose. The main areas of work they are statutorily obliged to undertake are work with children and work created by the Mental Health Act 1959. Add to this the uncertainty social workers themselves feel about what is the appropriate work of the social services departments and the whole area becomes a veritable minefield, with the discretion and predisposition of the individual social worker or team the deciding factors in determining who and what they deal with. In area teams, therefore, the individuals who act as initial filters, by referring to a more appropriate agency or deciding the applicant is at the appropriate agency to deal with his problem, stand in a crucial position in deciding the work load of the social services department* and other agencies: they act as a gatekeeper for their own agency and others. The ramifications of this are extensive and will be discussed in Chapter 5.

ASSESSMENT

After this initial filtering, which is often effected by reception staff, a second stage of the process is arrived at, when the applicant sees a social worker and presents their problem in greater detail. At this point a dialogue is entered into by social worker and applicant and a process of assessment begins. Referral to another agency is again a possible outcome. For example an applicant may approach the area team in connection with marital problems and it may be that, after discussion with the duty officer, some of the problems are clarified such that it is more appropriate for the case to be referred to a solicitor to institute divorce proceedings, or to a marriage guidance counsellor for marital work. Adequate assessment may, of course, be a process in itself comprising more than one interview, but from the point of initial contact with a social worker an assessment process is set in motion, the end result of which depends on a large number of variables – the first and foremost of which is whether the case is considered an appropriate one for the social services department. If it is, then some plan is made with the client; if not then the case may well be referred to another agency.

One problem here is that the social worker in this situation sees his primary task as assessment with a number of possible outcomes, but does not always explain this to the applicant, who often assumes that help is available and wants to know what it is, how he gets it, and from whom. This initial assessment stage is crucial, as it is here that wider ranging problems and those where there is potential for prevention can be detected, often at a stage when preventive work can achieve a lasting effect. Obvious examples include work with elderly clients where requests for help with a particular difficulty give rise to an opportunity to discuss a range of matters such as aids, finances, heating, and social clubs so that even if the client is not interested at that time they become aware of some of the provisions available and where to ask about them. By taking a wider view than dealing with a specific request, the social worker at the initial stage can play an educational/information/publicity role that may benefit the client in the future. Similarly, in cases of families with financial difficulties early intervention and thorough assessment may prevent more serious consequences such as fuel disconnections and eviction.

INITIAL SHORT-TERM MANAGEMENT

At the conclusion of the assessment process in the initial interview social worker and client have to come to some understanding about what future action, if any, is to be taken. The client's needs, having been established, have to be considered in relation to the resources the agency has at its disposal. At this point the relevant questions are those of how appropriate the nature of the referral is to the work of the social services department, whether there is another agency within whose province the referral more properly falls, or whether the problem is of a nature where there is no resolution or relevant agency and in effect the client's need is to ventilate his or her frustration. If it is the case that the problem would be more appropriately dealt with by another agency, then the intake worker will either facilitate this, or explain to the client how to go about it for themselves. For example, take a young mother in receipt of supplementary benefit needing a new mattress and bedding for the eldest of her three children, who is enuretic. The social worker may decide to write to the Department of Health and Social Security, putting the client's case and requesting an exceptional needs payment. Both social worker and client need to be clear about what is to be done, who is to do it, and the likely outcome.

Where a client is worried, perhaps, about an increase in the rent of their privately rented flat – once this has been established in the initial interview as the focus of concern – the client is likely to be advised to visit the rent officer as the person most appropriate to deal with the problem. In other cases the intake worker may want to make further enquiries, with the client's consent, to other agencies on the problem presented. For example, where a mother presents her 10-year-old son as becoming beyond her control, the intake worker is likely to want to contact the boy's school, the educational psychologists, and probably the health visitor if there are very young children in the family, to build up a wider picture of what is known about the child and family. The reasons for this need to be explained to the client who is then in a position to appreciate what action is being taken and why, and that any decision about work to be undertaken with the family will rest on a wide range of information and the views of different agencies.

A major factor in the initial short-term management stage of the intake process is that when the client leaves the office they should have a clear idea of what, if anything, the intake worker is going to do; why it is being done; and what to expect as the next stage. Thus the initial interview lays certain expectations and responsibilities on both worker and client, and both need to be clear about these. The intake senior social worker will probably briefly discuss the case with the worker while the client is in the office, so as to clarify what the response might be, given the existing priorities and work load of the intake team. Clients should be advised about the time which will probably elapse before a service is provided or a further contact from the worker can be expected, to avoid fruitless chasing up of requests and consequent frustration.

LONGER-TERM MANAGEMENT

Those cases that are not dealt with on a one-off basis or by being referred to another agency then require a decision to be made of the future involvement of the department, in the light of both client need and the resources and priorities of the agency. Intake worker and intake senior together need to discuss the case to clarify matters relating to the nature of future contact and questions of allocation. If the initial assessment has been adequate it should be possible to make at least preliminary decisions about what is required and what social work intervention would be appropriate. This may, in some cases, require further interviews with other family members or the whole family to establish more clearly the nature and parameters of the problem. A particularly common example of this is where adolescents present at intake saying they are unhappy at home, refuse to return, and ask to be received into care. Generally the obvious next stage is a family interview, and hence the case needs allocation for this to happen as soon as possible. Ideally, allocation would be directly to the worker who first saw the adolescent, as long as they were able to follow up quickly.

The intake-team model of organization facilitates flexibility such that most cases can be thus allocated. Other cases may be deemed suitable for short-term intervention by the intake team, possibly on a task-centred or contract basis. Some cases presented at intake are clearly of a long-term or chronic nature, and if the decision in the light of available resources is that the social services department should be involved, may be referred direct to a long-term team. In other cases, although clearly of a long-term nature, but where immediate action is required, it is generally unlikely that a long-term worker will be instantly available and an intake worker will need to deal with the immediate problem, transfer to long-term being effected subsequently at an appropriate stage in the development of the case. For example, where an intake worker has taken a Place of Safety Order on a young child the case may be appropriately transferred at the time of the court hearing.

There are, therefore, four major functions served by the intake process: filtering requests for service more appropriate to other agencies; initial assessment of client need at point of application; clarification of client need in terms of agency function and resources; and decision making concerning future contact with the agency in the light of the agency's priorities and client's need. All these functions take place against a background of inadequate resources and hence rationing procedures, both informal and formal, implicit and explicit. Alongside these four functions of the intake process are three necessary attributes for workers included in the process. Workers require a wide range of knowledge and experience of a variety of resources, both of their own and other agencies, to best decide which agency in the community is most available and appropriate to deal with the problem. The agency, at intake primarily reception and duty officer staff, and also as reflected in the general ethos of the whole team, needs to pay adequate attention to its 'public face' – reception and waiting room facilities – and should ideally provide a sympathetic environment and response to applicants, affording them the time and space to vent their feelings, problems, and grievances in an atmosphere where they will obtain some measure of acknowledgement. Finally, the object of the intake process should be to render assistance as appropriate to the client as soon as possible after the initial contact – the time when the client feels that the problem has become insurmountable and they cannot continue without outside intervention.

The intake process can, therefore, be seen as one of great complexity, involving an area team (primarily clerical/reception and duty officer staff) in making a series of decisions on individual applicant's approaches to the department, in the light of a set of criteria which may be decided upon at departmental policy level but which become operational at grass-roots intake level. The knowledge and skill required of the individual duty officer to function efficiently and effectively is considerable in view of the widely disparate roles social workers in local authority departments are expected to play, and expectations it is considered their brief to fulfil. The Service Delivery Study (DHSS 1975), undertaken by the DHSS in 1973, showed that it was often the clerical staff who were called upon to mediate the crucial first contact with an applicant assisted, with the implementation of a duty rota, by a duty officer. The role of duty officer was felt to be one of the most testing roles a social worker was called on to fulfil, in terms of the variety and quantity of problems presented. The authors state: 'what was very clear was that there must be a system for the rational disposal of cases and that the essential ingredients of such a system are professional support, ready access to resources and disciplined recording' (DHSS 1975: 7).

Intake, assessment, and initial allocation need be as speedy as possible. The shortfalls experienced by many teams in the efficiency and effectiveness of their intake process when organized into duty-rota systems incorporating most social workers in the team culminated in a growing impetus towards organizing so as to have a team of social workers with a remit to take on all new, crisis, and possibly short-term work – that is, towards developing intake teams.

The importance of reception and initial contacts

Younghusband (1978a) maintains that in the early 1970s it was still common practice in social services departments for an initial interview to be undertaken by clerical staff, before any contact with social work staff. Perlman (1960) distinguishes between the applicant and client phases – an applicant being the person who initially approaches the agency, only entering the client phase after there has been some definition of reciprocal roles and aims between applicant and social worker and a subsequent agreement to work together towards particular goals. Applicants approaching the agency are thus generally first seen by the receptionist. The role of receptionist is too often viewed as a lowly clerical task, and reception staff are rarely given any training in the organization and function of social services departments. Their task must have become even more complex immediately after the Seebohm reorganization when the public, professionals, and administrators were confused about the role and function of the new 'one door for all' social services departments. The result of the heavy bombardment of area teams after the Seebohm reorganization was that what amounted to rationing took place; that is, decisions were taken, often on an *ad hoc* basis, as to who would and would not be seen, and what was and was not appropriate work for social services departments. These decisions were, and sometimes still are, often made by a clerical officer on the applicant's first contact with the agency.

Reception tends to be viewed as a passive role, having little effect on the work of the agency – whereas the reverse would seem to be the case. The receptionist can act as an advocate or as a suppressor *vis-à-vis* an applicant being seen. It is usually the receptionist whom the applicant first sees on visiting the agency, and once the individual has decided to approach the social services department the attitude of the receptionist and the nature of the intake process are crucial in determining whether or not the contact with the department is maintained. The receptionist's attitude affects not only applicants but also social workers, in that often the receptionist makes an initial assessment and conveys this to the social worker, thereby possibly influencing the social worker's perception about the applicant. For example, take the implicit messages in the following two statements that may well be made by reception staff: 'Mrs Brown is very upset, I'll take her into an interview room rather than leave her in the waiting room' – this tends to imply that the social worker should hurry along to see Mrs Brown; on the other hand 'Mr Smith wants a bus pass, he's off work but there doesn't seem much wrong with him' seems to imply that Mr Smith can sit and wait and there's no rush to see him. Such observations on the part of reception staff are quite natural and often helpful, but serve to illustrate the crucial role of the receptionist for applicants.

Receptionists also protect social workers. For example, if a social worker is very busy and harassed the receptionist may divert difficult clients, try to regulate the bombardment, mediate between social worker and client, and make decisions about what is and what is not urgent. For the receptionist, the visiting applicant/client is ideally her prime responsibility, although other tasks such as filing and telephone calls often intervene, and her primary task is to facilitate contact between the social worker and the applicant/client. In the case of a client known to a particular social worker the task is relatively straightforward, but the job of the receptionist is made increasingly difficult when, as was and often still is the case, no social worker is committed to seeing new applicants – that is, when duty work is seen as a chore, high on nuisance value, and taking the social worker away from the 'real work' of seeing his own clients. An increased burden is thus placed on the receptionist to deal with, or redirect, the applicant and thereby free the duty officer from interviewing. Therefore, the initial interview, assessment, and decision making is effectively undertaken by the receptionist, and the crucial role played by reception staff is, therefore, a major consideration in discussion of internal team organization.

As many studies have shown, the applicant's first contact with the agency is potentially crucial. This very often signifies that the problem for the individual has become a crisis and they have decided to seek help. Even where the request is for a particular service, such as welfare aids or straightforward advice, the first contact with the agency is likely to colour subsequent contacts and· serve to encourage or discourage the individual from approaching the agency when in need in the future. Sainsbury and Nixon (1979), in a study sponsored by the Department of Health and Social Security in 1975 in the Sheffield area into the content of family social work undertaken by the local authority social services department, the probation service, and the local Family Service Unit, found from the comments of clients that their first contact with whichever agency and whether in their own home, the office, or elsewhere, was nearly always accompanied by heightened feelings. When the first contact was at the agency, the agency itself provided the most vivid memory. Such factors as quality of reception, the attitude and manner of any staff encountered casually, and the nature of waiting room facilities may well all have a decisive influence on the subsequent contact with the social worker.

Mayer and Timms, in their study of client attitudes towards a social work agency, comment that 'it is only desperation that makes it possible to assume the role of client with self-respect' (Mayer and Timms 1970: 53). Reith (1975), in a study of people who sought social work help for the first time but did not continue the contact, found three common characteristics of those who refer themselves to a social work agency: they are anxious about their problem, they are uncertain about the agency's function and services, and they are apprehensive about the reception they will receive. This serves to emphasize the sensitivity required in dealing with individuals at their first contact with a social work agency, in what for them is often a novel and distasteful experience. Reith found that clients appreciated social workers who quickly put them at ease, and gave a brief explanation of the functions of the agency.

All too often social workers expect clients to be familiar with the social work game and the client role they are expected to assume. Reith suggested, as a result of his study, that: 'the intake service is crucial in any agency and must be upgraded from being an unwelcome chore and distraction' (Reith 1975: 69). Clients appear to place a high value on social workers who take a business-like approach to problems and their resolution and who demonstrate concern and competence and an ability to put the client at ease. In a study by Barker (1975) of clients' likes and dislikes, many clients' comments reflected the importance placed on the relationship established between social worker and client. This relationship was considered important not only in long-term work but also in one-off interviews which were often experienced by clients as therapeutic in themselves.

The importance of teamwork

One of the major characteristics of intake teams once in operation is their group cohesion. This is partly because intake workers are more often in the office as a result of the nature of their work than long-term workers, who spend a large proportion of their time either visiting clients in care or visiting families at home. Intake teams depend largely on work coming to the office, at least in the first instance. Also, due to the flow of work in intake and the worker's frequent role as 'middleman', much more administrative work is likely to have to be done in terms of liaison by telephone, memo writing, information seeking, and the like. Hence, intake-team workers are more likely to be in closer day-to-day contact with each other than long-term team members.

However, as Spencer (1973) points out in an article on the role of 'support' in social work, when individuals are continually faced with anxiety-provoking and often insoluble situations, which either they as a profession claim to be able to do something about, or which the general public expect them to do something about – a position that is particularly characteristic of an intake-team social worker – they need a high level of support from colleagues. Of this, Spencer says: 'Essentially support comes about by acceptance, by recognition, by understanding, by the reassurance that if I was in the same position as you, I would be doing the same thing' (Spencer 1973: 7). Of the various mechanisms social work organizations have devised to provide such support, the major one seems to be the work team, followed by supervisory and consultative machinery. Social workers place great importance on their work team, in terms of how well they get on with colleagues and the opportunities the team provides for discussing and sharing anxieties about cases. In one piece of research Spencer found that 80 per cent of social workers questioned said they discussed their cases with colleagues 'quite a lot' or 'a great deal'.

Prodgers (1979), in an article looking specifically at how intake workers cope with stress, points out that because of the pressures of intake work intake-team members need to feel that their colleagues are behind them and that there are others around to call on in times of crisis. Informal groups therefore play an important role in helping individuals cope with stress, and such groups evolve group norms and may, for example, sanction defensive reactions on the part of social workers. Such group cohesion can have negative as well as positive effects, and these will be discussed in Chapter 4. Prodgers suggests that one of the ways intake teams maintain their internal cohesion is by their attitude towards other agencies. He paints a picture of intake teams having what could be described as a 'siege mentality', feeling themselves to be constantly under pressure from external pressures, and hence developing a generalized antagonism towards other agencies. Whilst this is not necessarily always the case it is noticeable that at times of high demand or periods of staff shortages there seems to be an increased anger or hostility towards external agencies, DHSS and Housing generally being the targets of attacks – often, but not always, justifiably so. Other professionals, however, such as GPs and magistrates also come in for a number of attacks. Such antagonism directed towards external agencies and individuals, even if wrongly directed, serves to increase the cohesion of the intake group and tends to be particularly apparent when the group is under great pressure.

Marsh (1974), in a paper on the importance of teamwork in social work practice, suggests that social work managers, teachers, and social workers themselves have a poor understanding of this, perhaps because social work has traditionally had an individualist rather than a team ethic. In the case of intake teams it is necessary for the group to function as a cohesive and mutually supportive unit, and owing to the nature of work there is usually a high degree of sharing of knowledge, information, and cases, some clients becoming known to most members of the team at one time or another. As Marsh says 'because the job the team is called on to perform requires more than the sum of individual skills and aptitudes, a collection of capable individuals does not necessarily make a capable team' (Marsh 1974: 726). He points out that establishing a team does not necessarily produce teamwork, and discusses seven general characteristics of teamwork, all of which are relevant to the establishment of intake teams.

Firstly, team members must understand, and be committed to, team objectives. For intake workers these are to provide an assessment service, crisis service, and short-term social work service to new clients, and to see these tasks as their prime responsibility.

Secondly, members of a team are interdependent in skills and resources, because the job of the team requires more skill and knowledge than any one member could offer. Given the incredible variety of work dealt with by intake teams, there is a very high level of interdependence in the sharing of knowledge and skills, and individuals who find it difficult to ask for help and advice from colleagues are likely to experience substantial difficulties in trying to deal effectively – without tremendous waste of time and effort – with the variety of problems that clients present.

Thirdly, leadership and authority are participative, influence being exerted by different members depending upon the situation. Although intake workers are responsible to one or more senior social workers in line-management terms, because of the need for intake workers to take quick decisions, often during crises but also in response to requests for specific services, exclusive dependence on the senior social worker is dysfunctional and the group and individual worker take a high level of responsibility for their own decisions, often discussing a case and sharing in decisions, calling on different members' experience, skill, and knowledge.

Fourthly, teams should ideally operate flexibly and creatively in response to changing demands, such that procedures can be changed as required, and decisions about changes made on a team basis. Intake teams are obviously bound, to a large extent, by departmental policy and procedure, but within their own sphere of operation often have a fair degree of flexibility of their internal organization and procedures. Without such flexibility the intake team system would suffer from being unable to organize effectively to cope with the demands made upon it, and so the advantages supposed to accrue from such organization would be lost. Rigid management styles either from central management or the team leader are likely to militate against commitment to the team and to the team task, to the disadvantage of both the agency and the client.

The team needs a positive emotional climate to allow openness, trusting relationships, and free communication within the team. This again relates back to the individual social worker's need for emotional support when continually placed in potentially stressful situations and the need to share knowledge, skills, information, and anxieties to facilitate efficient and effective functioning as a team. When communication between team members if not open and trust in relationships is lacking, the team ceases to function as a team, individuals pursue their own ends, and the consequent anger, frustration, and lowering of morale affects not only team members but also the service to clients.

Effective teamwork tends to result in the team becoming more autonomous within the organization. Strong intake teams may develop considerable autonomy from the rest of the area team, but although they require a degree of autonomy to function, if the team becomes too autonomous the effects on the rest of the area team can be far-reaching and fundamental, for the intake team is dependent for its success and ability to sustain itself on its relationship with the rest of the area team. This will be discussed at greater length in the following chapter; it is sufficient to say here that a degree of autonomy for the intake team is necessary and valuable, but if carried too far can severely affect the rest of the area team's functioning.

Finally, the number of members in the team is controlled by the needs of the job. Marsh concludes that, given these central and very significant characteristics of teamwork, often not enough care and sophistication is practised in team selection; this has far-reaching results for the team affected. Selection of a good social worker but unsuitable team member will cost the team and department dearly. Such considerations obviously also apply to the selection of long-term team members but owing to the increased group cohesion and interdependence characteristic of intake teams, they seem especially pertinent to the selection of intake-team social workers.

The relationship between intake and long-term teams

Intake teams, as has been said before, cannot be viewed in isolation from the rest of the area team. Intake teams are usually not geographically based, servicing the whole catchment area of the area team. Long-term teams are generally organized so as to cover particular geographical patches, but may alternatively be organized along specialist lines – teams for the under-fives, adolescents, elderly, etc. – or work may be passed through to long-term senior social workers who allocate work among those staff they supervise, the only shared feature of such teams being their supervising senior.

For this organizational structure to function effectively there must be a clear system by which work is allocated and transferred, such that the flow of work from intake to long-term is relatively smooth. For this to be possible, the whole area team must be committed to this way of working. This is obviously particularly crucial at the time when an intake team is first being considered and set up. Unless most of the area team staff are either committed to the organization of social workers into intake and long-term teams, or are at least willing to attempt organization for a trial period, the system stands little chance of success. For an intake team to function effectively and be able to handle the incoming new and short-term work it is vital that it has the co-operation of long-term workers in taking over long-term cases once the decision has been made that a particular case is more appropriately handled by a long-term rather than intake worker.

If this commitment and co-operation is not forthcoming then the intake team rapidly grinds itself to a standstill, since more and more referrals come in and – while most of these can probably be dealt with on a one-off or short-term basis – a proportion will require long-term work. If these cases cannot be passed through to long-term teams then the intake workers are left carrying long-term cases as well as trying to function as an effective intake worker, resulting in neither role being adequately performed, with all the inherent problems and ramifications found under duty-rota systems. Consequently, it is crucial that not only the intake workers but the whole area team have a clear understanding of, and commitment to, the intake/long-term model of organization.

The deployment of staff between teams is related to the philosophy of the area team as to how work is to be handled. In the past there has tended to be the assumption, not always specified, that cases were closed only when either a satisfactory solution was found or the client died. Responsibility seemed to lie with the agency to provide a service rather than with the client to make positive use of it. This was clearly unrealistic and resulted in social workers' caseloads being full of long-term cases where there was no goal or plan of work, and often little that could be achieved.

One of the most common examples of this sort of practice was the caseloads of workers from the pre-Seebohm reorganization Welfare Departments, often carried on after 1971, often having 200 or more elderly and physically handicapped clients on their caseload. Clearly the social worker could not be working with this number of clients, and the contact often amounted to nothing more than popping in for a few minutes once or twice a year. Whilst some clients valued this as a useful point of contact should they want to discuss or request something, it constituted a drastic waste of manpower in a service constantly complaining of being unable to cope with the pressure of demands to which it is subjected. In addition, when a case is 'open' and 'allocated' to an individual social worker, although perhaps no work is actually being undertaken and no real service provided (which may have been agreed by the social worker and senior), the fact that it is an allocated case tends to contribute to the overwhelming pressure felt by many social workers.

More recently many teams' caseloads, both long-term and short-term, are being examined much more closely and decisions about whether or not to allocate are being taken in the light of such considerations as the client's willingness to use the help offered, the ability of the worker and the agency to help in the resolution of the problem, the appropriateness of the case to the social services department, and a close scrutiny of the meaning of 'support' in different cases. In a world where supply falls far short of demand, and resources in terms of staff are never likely to be adequate, it is necessary for long-term and intake teams to make hard decisions, cut their losses, and use their time, skills, and resources economically and with the most effect.

Duncan (1973), in discussing the setting up of an intake team in 1971, found that where it was the policy of intake workers to follow through the short-term and crisis work they were undertaking on duty, they spent much more time on the initial assessment and many problems were resolved without necessitating a further call to the office, whereas under the earlier duty-rota system often only brief details were taken from the client at their initial interview and the case then passed through for allocation. Consequently, before the establishment of the intake team only 30 per cent of referrals were dealt with on a short-term basis but after the intake team was set up over 60 per cent of referrals were dealt with in this way.

Goldberg *et al.* (1978) found that the outstanding feature in long-term work was the concentration on surveillance and review visiting. This was noted in 75 per cent of all long-term cases and was said to be the most important social work activity in 40 per cent of cases. In over 50 per cent of the long-term cases surveyed the social worker expected no change and said that the cases would remain open indefinitely. Consequently, chronically disturbed and disorganized families take up a vast amount of social work time and are usually on long-term workers' caseloads. It has been suggested that one of the reasons for this is that intake teams tend not to work with families with early manifestations of family breakdown, at a point when preventive work may be beneficial, resulting in families being chronically disrupted by the time they are on a long-term worker's caseload, with little possibility of achieving any major changes in the family's functioning.

In another study of the same area office undertaken by Goldberg and Fruin (1976), the differing styles of intervention and general philosophy underlying social work practices are highlighted by the differing expectations of social workers with essentially similar caseloads; one social worker expected all of his cases to be open after three years while another worker expected only 34 per cent to be open after three years. The first worker could be described as suffering from 'long-term mentality', resulting in a relatively static caseload with very limited ability to take on any new work; the second worker can be assumed to be working in a more structured way, planning and prepared to close long-term cases in which either some resolution or none is arrived at.

However, since 1973 an unvarying 70 per cent of cases which survive the intake stage are estimated to be open three years or more later, despite changes in the prevailing ethos of the team, such as to cut back long-term caseloads or undertake more short-term pieces of work with allocated clients. This steady 70 per cent probably reflects, at least in part, the fact that a high proportion of long-term work is made up of statutory child-care cases. Hence whatever the prevailing ethos of the team these cases will still have to be allocated, and because of the responsibility of social services departments towards children in care these cases are likely to be ranked as high priority in any allocation system. This then leaves long-term workers with less available time to take on non-statutory cases such as the follow-up of mentally ill clients coming out of hospital and the mentally handicapped; the decline in specialist skills further contributes to the poor quality of service to these groups.

Long-term teams, therefore, also have to carefully scrutinize their caseloads and decide priorities about allocation. Their decisions need to be clear to intake workers, since the sorts of cases that the long-term team affords low priority are obviously less likely to be allocated. If, for example, the long-term team decided they were giving only low priority to counselling parents with mentally handicapped children, there would be little point in an intake worker encouraging a parent to seek help from social services in such a situation, for no such help will be readily available from a long-term worker. The alternative is to look outside to the voluntary agencies for support. Where intake and long-term workers regularly move between teams this gives an opportunity for cross-fertilization and can encourage long-term workers to try short-term or task-centred pieces of work, hence overcoming the rather static 'long-term mentality' trap which some workers fall into.

However, such movement of staff also causes difficulties for agency staff and clients in terms of the necessary redistribution of caseloads. However, there is no point in intake teams taking a firm line on the closure of cases where they feel nothing can be usefully achieved if long-term workers are not equally rigorous.

The two areas of difficulty most often raised when intake and long-term teams are discussed as the model for an area team are those of élitism and the problems in transferring cases through to long-term teams. Corrie (1976), in her survey of all London Boroughs with intake teams, found that all but one of the intake teams surveyed functioned apart from the rest of the area team, and 50 per cent of teams agreed that this tended to lead to exclusiveness. Gostick (1976), in a survey of data over a 16-month period after an intake team had been established, found that although the referral rate increased steadily, a corresponding number of cases were closed immediately, and that although there was a steadily accumulating work load in intake the number of cases referred to long-term teams was relatively static.

Intake workers, therefore, appeared to respond to the increased referral rate by closing cases faster and thereby increasing their own work flow while protecting the long-term workers from the increased pressure. Gostick related this to the élitist nature often ascribed to intake teams. As the initial organizational effectiveness of intake teams in containing increased referral rates became apparent, so more social work resources were channelled into intake teams. Hence intake teams have tended to increase in size, develop in expertise, and contain more and more new referrals, and in so doing they have become more insular and self-contained. Clearly, small intake teams – perhaps without their own senior – are much more dependent on other staff in the area team for their day-to-day functioning. The larger the team the more autonomous it is able to become. Some degree of polarization between teams seems almost inevitable, but when an 'us and them' attitude becomes entrenched there is the danger of communication between the teams breaking down. The consequence, particularly where intake workers take on something of an élitist stance, placing greatest importance on short-term work, is that long-term workers do not close cases because there is little work coming through from intake.

Correspondingly, to contain the referrals in intake, intake workers undertake an increased proportion of the work themselves, often doing little more than offering the client information and advice. This results in a deterioration in the service to clients, while administratively the system appears efficient because more work is being dealt with by the intake team, and if long-term workers are not closing cases, the total caseload of the area is increasing. Polarization, and the friction that can subsequently develop, is therefore an inherent problem in this model of organization, but the potential adverse effects can be minimized by introducing features which ensure a degree of cross-fertilization, such as long-term workers taking over when the intake team have a meeting, other seniors occasionally acting as duty senior, and frequent area meetings for the whole area team, where problems can be openly discussed.

The second problem characteristic of intake/long-term team organization is the difficulty of transferring cases from intake to long-term teams. In the early days of the establishment of intake teams one of the fears often expressed was that intake workers would lose their skills for long-term work, and many intake workers kept a few long-term cases to 'keep their hand in'. More recently the opposite fear has been expressed – that intake workers deal with all the exciting crisis and short-term work where preventive potential is greatest, while long-term workers are left with all the chronic and intractable cases.

Long-term workers, therefore, often express the desire to do some short-term work, to lift the burden of their long-term cases. Theoretically, this is both understandable and easily accommodated, in that most intake workers would be quite happy for a long-term worker to deal with a few short-term cases. However, in reality, much of the work the intake team deals with needs to be taken up quickly – indeed, this was one of the reasons behind the development of intake teams. Long-term workers, therefore, have to be prepared to take on a case at short notice, and if this is during a crisis to be available at the point of crisis – for example, be able to go out to visit when a school rings and says one of their children is badly bruised, or when a doctor rings and wants a social worker to visit someone who is behaving very strangely and perhaps dangerously. Invariably, long-term workers do not have this flexibility because of the demands of their long-term cases, and the response is often 'I'll have some space in x weeks'. Consequently, whatever the reason – whether it be pressure of work or the famous 'long-term mentality' – the intake team is often the only team organized sufficiently flexibly, and with sufficient experience, to deal with nearly all new short-term and crisis work from the outset.

For short-term work there is relatively little difficulty; the intake worker is expected to undertake this. However, even in this area situations may change and what was initially seen as a problem that could be resolved in a three-month period may turn into a complex family situation including, for example, the removal of children and possible court proceedings. Likewise many crises, especially those affecting children, are clearly likely to require attention over a fairly lengthy period. The intake worker is then faced with the problem of transferring the case to the appropriate long-term team. Twenty-two out of the thirty-two questionnaire replies received by Corrie (1976) spoke of problems in transferring cases from intake to long-term teams. These seemed to centre on the lack of staff, particularly qualified and experienced staff, in long-term teams.

There is rarely a continuous smooth flow of work. If there is relatively little work being transferred by the intake team then long-term workers are less likely to review and close their own cases as there is no pressure on them to take on more. Conversely, if there is a great deal of work to be transferred from intake to long-term teams the latter cannot take it all on at once and the system becomes clogged. Intake workers know they are unlikely to get a case allocated to a long-term worker and so respond to the pressure on them by dealing with more new referrals on a one-off basis, being even more neglectful of the wider or underlying difficulties because they have no time to deal with any more cases, since they are already dealing with too many medium and long-term ones.

Other elements also feature in the likelihood or not of cases being transferred, such as the intake worker's reluctance to transfer the case, and the desire of both intake and long-term workers to shape their caseloads in particular ways. Whatever the agreement, it is crucial that all staff clearly know how cases are transferred, who is responsible for the final decision to allocate or not, and who is responsible for a case while it is awaiting allocation. If these matters are not settled and explicit there is endless friction and confusion as to who takes responsibility, which is related to organizational and administrative pressures rather than client need. There are also professional anxieties about the wisdom of transferring cases. For example, the intake worker may have had the benefit of working with the family in a crisis when there is an increased possibility of change, and the long-term worker may feel he cannot affect the family now the impetus of the crisis has been lost. The intake worker is likely to have worked towards mitigating some of the presenting problems and hence, although he may feel the family need further help, this may not be as clear to either the family or the long-term worker.

Clients and workers sometimes find it difficult to end relationships or transfer to another worker and it is important that clients understand the organization of the teams at an early stage so that they do not develop unrealistic expectations that they will always have the same social worker. The difficulties of transferring cases are impossible to wholly overcome but their divisive effect can be minimized by there being clear guidelines on how responsibility is divided in the interim period, the fostering of good relationships between the intake and long-term teams, and flexibility and good will on all sides. Ensuring some feedback from long-term to intake teams to highlight any inconsistencies in assessment between the two teams is also worthwhile.

The relationships between intake and long-term teams can be seen to be crucial to the effective working of such a model. Where relationships are poor or break down there is the danger of intake and long-term teams working side by side in the agency but with each having their own goals and objectives. Unless a similar general ethos is shared by all members of the agency, they may possibly be working at cross-purposes, and the intake/long-term division could become unbreachable.

4

The nature of intake work

Introduction

Intake teams were established with the objective of providing an
efficient, sympathetic, and uniform service to clients, and as a means
of overcoming the difficulties encountered in handling new work
after reorganization, such as the long waiting lists for social work
visits, the paucity of informed and available information and advice,
and the wide diversity of responses from different social workers to
very similar problems. Intake teams have, therefore, by virtue of
their location within the organizational structure of social services
departments, tended to move away from traditional models of social
work practice and to develop their own particular styles.

Intake teams have been criticized for the problem-focused nature
of their work, which has been viewed as encouraging the tendency to
look only at the presenting problem, deal with the immediate
difficulty, and avoid the other underlying and contributory factors.
Likewise, the concern of many intake teams to offer a relatively
consistent service to the public has been viewed as providing a uniform
service at the expense of a sympathetic one. In both the problem-
focus of intake work and the goals of offering a relatively uniform
and consistent service, intake teams are accused of prematurely
categorizing clients' problems and then offering standardized solutions. This implies that administrative efficiency and expediency
take over from the quality of service offered to clients as the criteria
for success and as the criteria for job satisfaction for the worker.

Intake workers function as front-line practitioners and as such have to deal with a tremendous diversity of demands, with a questionable capacity to mediate the demands made upon them. As such, there are pressures that are particular to intake by virtue of its location, and team cohesion is critical in helping members withstand such pressure. The ethos of the team has wide-ranging implications and can function to either facilitate or thwart the quality of service available to clients. The intake model, therefore, creates a series of problems by virtue of the nature of intake work. However, teams that are aware of and alert to the dangers can do much to overcome them, and the criticisms levelled at intake teams cannot be considered exclusive to that model of organization.

Intake as a problem-focused service

Most intake workers generally believe that the vast majority of new referrals are of people with specific material needs. This is a marked contrast to the general ethos of social work practice in the 1960s and early 1970s, when great store was set by identifying the factors underlying the 'presenting problem'. The standard caricature of social work practice was that any client requesting help with, for example, their fuel bills must necessarily have deep-seated emotional problems and it is these that should be the focus of social work intervention – the bills being of little importance, and used by the client only to gain social work help. Likewise any families with debt problems, it was thought, necessarily required marital casework. To give a specific example, a social worker dealing with a Turkish-Cypriot single parent and her four sons went to great lengths to discuss the emotional, symbolic, and cultural meaning of the youngest son's circumcision and when this was completed closed the case, merely commenting that the mother did not seem to be receiving enough money to live on, was being charged an extortionate rent by her private landlord, and that the state of the property was extremely dangerous and totally inadequate to the family's needs. These latter matters the social worker saw as no concern of hers even to advise the client about, let alone help in resolving. Whereas, therefore, one of the traditional criticisms of social work has been that it has tended to concentrate on intra-personal and inter-personal problems at the expense of dealing with requests for specific material services, the opposite charge can now be made against intake work.

The whole ethos of intake teams tends to be to deal with the problem presented, often a request for a particular service, and then to close the case. There is thus always the danger that longer-term underlying problems are neither identified nor examined. Prodgers (1979) found that most intake workers he interviewed admitted that because of the pressures on them, such as it being a hectic day with clients queuing in the waiting room to be seen and a lot of telephoning and letter writing in relation to the day's referrals awaiting, they often did not investigate problems other than the immediate one presented by the client. Often, even where the worker becomes aware of other problems, he may blinker himself to the full importance of these, making a conscious effort to deal only with the presenting problem.

Shaw (1979) sees the establishment of specialist intake teams as highlighting certain areas of concern, for whereas all systems must operate some form of intake process, certain issues tend to be clouded in more diffuse systems, only clearly emerging as a focus for concern once a specialized intake-team system is in operation. Commenting on the business-like approach adopted by intake workers in dealing with clients and problems, he sees this approach as contributing to the rapid identification and specification of needs to be met and problems to be tackled. While such action may be wholly warranted there is a danger of premature categorization, arising out of the anxiety of the worker to make some sense of the client and his problems. Such premature categorization may cause the worker to lose out on gaining a broader perspective on the client and his difficulties. The worker may also try to impose their assessment onto the client so that both are in agreement about the nature of the problem, whereas the client might have quite different views about the problem and its possible resolution. Inherent in the emphasis in intake of specifying needs, agreeing goals, defining tasks, and agreeing on contracts, is the risk of focusing solely on practicalities and service delivery issues to the exclusion of less-tangible forms of help which may be equally important to the client, if not more so.

The classic ideals of intake systems – rapid response and efficient service – need to remain compatible with humane endeavour and working with clients' feelings. It is often suggested that the traditional job satisfaction social workers found in their long-term work with families tends to be replaced in intake workers by their seeing how much they can achieve with clients in the shortest possible time. Work undertaken may, therefore, be more rushed and less well performed as a direct result of the organizational structure within which the worker finds himself. Titcomb (1974), referring to this particular problem, cites the importance of intake workers learning to limit their caseloads rather than lower their casework standards. This, however, is easier said than done. In an organizational structure consisting of an intake and one or more long-term teams, the long-term teams are more or less effectively protected from the immediate impact of client bombardment by the presence of the intake team, whose function it invariably is to deal with all new and short-term incoming work. The intake team, however, is afforded no such protection, except by the responses to clients of reception and switchboard staff as discussed in Chapter 3. Furthermore, if it is accepted that many problems presented to intake teams are requests for a specific service, they often need rapid attention and resolution, as does the crisis work generally presented at intake.

Given these considerations it becomes clear how difficult it can be to relieve the pressure on intake workers and hence alleviate the less desirable results of this in social work practice. When under pressure it is much easier for the intake worker to concentrate on one particular problem and try to resolve this than to undertake a wider-ranging assessment process which is likely to uncover other problems. The results of Reith's study (1975) of people who sought social work help for the first time suggested that clients prefer a business-like approach to the problem and its resolution from a person who demonstrates concern, competence, and an ability to put the client at ease. Thus while general relationship skills are valued, it is the competence to deal with the problem presented that is particularly important to clients. At the time of the setting up of intake teams many social workers expressed the fear that intake teams might tend to function as an automated mechanistic process, pushing clients through the intake system, categorizing the problem, offering some solution, and closing the case, without using the traditional social work skills of forming and utilizing relationships. This is clearly not generally the case and interpersonal skills are as important in intake work as in long-term social work practice. Whilst intake work tends to be relatively highly problem-focused, the ability of the intake worker to establish relationships with clients is of considerable importance in facilitating work undertaken and determining outcomes.

Goldberg *et al.* (1977), studied one year's intake work of an area team in Southampton, where the intake team consisted of five full-time and one part-time social workers, a part-time advisor for the disabled, and one senior social worker to cover a population of 73,000. There was an average of 200 referrals per week. They found that since the formation of the intake team, which aimed at dealing primarily with explicit requests on a short-term basis unless there were clear indications for long-term work such as with a child in care or a highly vulnerable elderly person, approximately 75 per cent of all incoming cases were closed within two months, clients being encouraged to re-refer themselves when future difficulties arose. The intake team emerged as a 'service delivery' team which aimed at undertaking a particular piece of work with a client, the responsibility lying with the client to pursue particular goals.

Three types of request commonly made to intake teams were distinguished: requests for information and advice, requests for specific services, and requests for investigation of particular situations. 40 per cent of all cases in the area studied were requesting a specific service, rising to 76 per cent among the elderly and physically handicapped. However, approximately 25 per cent of cases were closed on the day of referral and five months after the end of the study only 6 per cent of cases referred were still receiving continuous social work help from the point of original referral. 47 per cent of cases were closed within one week of referral, 64 per cent within one month, and 81 per cent within three months. Thus, if the intake team were working to a definition of short-term work – work expected to take no more than three months – the intake team alone would be dealing with approximately 80 per cent of the incoming work, the other 20 per cent being dealt with either by an intake worker initially and then transferred to a long-term worker or else allocated straight to a long-term worker. Long-term teams may, therefore, be wholly unaware of 80 per cent of the work coming in to the area team. Of the types of work undertaken by the intake team, exploration and assessment was recorded in over 75 per cent of all cases, giving information and advice in 50 per cent of cases, and mobilization of resources in over 33 per cent of cases. Casework – that is, what is viewed as the traditional social work activity – was recorded in only 20 per cent of all cases. A fairly clear picture thus emerges of intake workers offering a service consisting of giving information and advice, practical help, inter-agency liaison, and general assessment activities.

Neill *et al.* (1976) studying the changes in perceptions of social workers in four area offices between 1972 and 1975 found that one of the most noticeable changes was in caseload size. The number of cases allocated to long-term workers decreased by approximately 38 per cent between 1972 and 1975, and even in the client groups where there were the highest number of allocated cases – children, the elderly, and the physically handicapped – the number of cases allocated had decreased. Even fewer mentally ill or mentally handicapped cases were allocated in 1975 than in 1972. One of the causes of this decrease in numbers of allocated cases was seen to be the establishment of intake teams in these areas, resulting in much of the incoming work being dealt with on a short-term, problem-focused basis and, therefore, not being allocated to long-term workers. Whilst in many ways this probably constitutes an improvement in service in that cases do not so readily add to workers' caseloads while no work is being planned and undertaken, it does tend to mean that the cases passed through to long-term teams are more likely to be those where there is some statutory responsibility, as otherwise many cases are dealt with on a short-term basis by intake workers and then closed. Consequently, those groups and individuals for whom there is little or no statutory responsibility and who do not tend to present themselves to social services are less likely to receive social work help. Most obvious among such groups are the mentally ill and handicapped, traditionally a low priority for social services provision and unlikely to fare any better under a system of organization that depends largely on problems being presented at intake and dealt with largely on a short-term basis.

Results of the research undertaken by Goldberg *et al.* (1977) and Glampson and Goldberg (1976) confirm the impression that social services departments are increasingly being used by the public as information and advice agencies, and for specific service provision. Goldberg *et al.* found that intake workers spent most of their time as follows: screening incoming demands; providing practical help, especially to the elderly and physically handicapped; acting as a sort of Citizens Advice Bureau; and finally filling advocacy functions, especially in social security and housing matters. In a random sample of consumers taken by Goldberg *et al.* the elderly and physically handicapped emerged as the group who were most satisfied with the service they received, and also the group who received the most practical help. The consumer survey showed that alongside this group clients who approached social services with financial and housing problems emerged as equally satisfied in that their expectations were fulfilled; they wanted and received information and advice.

Glampson and Goldberg (1976) made similar findings in their comparison of consumer research between 1972 and 1975. Whereas in 1972 the degree of satisfaction felt by consumers had been largely uniform, in 1975 the most satisfied were the elderly and handicapped and those who had housing and financial problems – that is, those groups who received basically practical help.

There seemed by 1975 to be emerging on the part of the public a conception of social services departments as general information and advice centres. Of interest in relation to this is a study recently undertaken by Corney (1979) comparing social work undertaken in a general-practice setting to that in an intake team. Clients referred to the general-practitioner attachment scheme were found to be more representative of the area served in terms of housing tenure, financial situation, and employment status, than those referred to the intake team. The latter group of clients contained a higher than average proportion who were unemployed, living on benefits, or in council or rented accommodation. In the attachment scheme a greater number of referrals centred on emotional problems or problems due to psychiatric illness, usually depression. Fewer emotional problems were referred to intake teams, where many referrals related to housing, financial, and practical problems. The rapid 'one-off' intervention and quick closing characteristic of intake teams was evident; 33 per cent of all cases were dealt with the same day and 70 per cent within a month, cases being closed at or shortly after the last contact.

Contrastingly, in the attachment scheme the length of contact was much longer and cases were kept open after the last contact. This must be largely because of the different types of cases dealt with by the two teams. One-off intervention is clearly more likely in a case where the client was having problems getting his social security benefit which will be rapidly dealt with and closed than where the client has been referred suffering from post-puerperal depression.

Corney points out (Corney 1979) that attachment-scheme social workers kept up contact longer and offered greater continuity of service and had a lower re-referral rate than intake workers. This ignores the fact that social workers in settings other than intake have greater opportunities to regulate their work flow, since they are largely dependent on other professionals rather than direct client requests for their work. They can, therefore, regulate referrals in a way not open to intake workers, except in extreme situations, and are less likely to undertake crisis and emergency statutory work. It was also suggested that intake workers tend to work more in isolation from their referral agents and hence feel less responsibility towards them. Such characteristics obviously vary, but are not inherent to intake-team organization. To the contrary, a well-established and committed intake team is likely to have good inter-agency links in its area and is indeed dependent on these to function effectively.

Intake teams clearly emerge as offering primarily a problem-focused service to clients. This has both positive and negative ramifications for social work objectives and client need. Rees (1974), in a study of the experiences of eight sets of clients and their respective social workers, defines 'contact' as to: 'refer to meetings between social workers and clients which are flirting and fleeting in nature, transitory, not having much effect on a client's problem, their appreciation of the social worker's identity, their understanding of his job or their conception of themselves' (Rees 1974: 256). Certainly a proportion of the contacts between intake workers and clients are of this nature, the intake worker being no more or less than any of a series of other agency officials the client runs into in the course of his week. What tends to be the intake ethos militates against the building up of a deep relationship with the client. This ethos consists of accepting a case; undertaking a piece of work with the client, be it helping the client negotiate with other agencies, helping him decide whether to apply for residential care, or counselling after a marital breakdown; and then closing the case after a short period of intervention. Clients thus tend to be presented with a series of choices, the decision and outcome being their responsibility.

Under such a system the client who either cannot articulate his need or who finds it difficult to make or sustain contact with agencies is likely to receive little or no service. One of the criticisms levelled at intake teams is that they tend not to work preventively. Being problem-focused they wait until problems are brought to them, deal with specific episodes and then encourage the individual or family to re-refer themselves as and when future problems arise; early manifestations of family stress are, therefore, rarely dealt with, as is often also the case with non-material problems of the elderly. The ability of intake teams to undertake preventive work is determined not only by the organizational position of the team – for it could be argued that intake teams are in a prime position to undertake such work, being able to encourage referrals of early manifestations of family stress – but also by the availability of staff time and the availability of long-term workers to take on certain cases.

If intake teams were to rigorously prune the tasks they were currently called on to perform, and take explicit team decisions not (for example) to deal with information and advice matters where there are other agencies able to undertake this work, then they would be in a better position to direct their energies and resources to those areas of work when an input of short-term work at an early stage would be expected to have high preventive potential. Such a shift in emphasis would require the re-education of other agencies, professions, and the public away from the image of social services as an agency giving advice and information and towards the early referral of family problems. If freed of such an image intake teams may be able to play a key preventive role both with individuals and families and in identifying newly emergent problems, which are likely to be first presented to intake teams once they have reached the stage of being articulated and outside help sought. Consequently, although criticisms can be levelled at the problem-focus of intake teams, these are not necessarily inherent to intake organization and are rather dependent on matters such as the deployment of staff throughout the area team and the necessity of establishing a clear and shared understanding as to how the whole team views its role and function.

Intake teams and the uniformity of service

Theoretically, intake teams were developed as an organizational response to the confusion and poor level of service often found in duty-rota systems after the Seebohm reorganization. The formation of intake teams was expected to result in the delivery of an efficient, sympathetic, and uniform service. Whereas previously there had evidently been a wide diversity of responses to the problems presented to area teams – depending on a wide variety of factors, including the training, experience, and personal preference of the duty officer, which would be related to which of the specialized departments they had worked in before the Seebohm reorganization – the formation of intake teams was seen as a means of offering a more consistent service. Intake teams of themselves would not achieve this end but, as a result of the greater cohesion of such groups, they tend to develop a group ethos as to how work is dealt with, which can have positive and negative effects.

Given the crucial gatekeeper role of intake workers in deciding who does and who does not receive help, it seems highly advisable that there should be some degree of consistency in the decisions that are taken so that the public receive an equable service. At the extreme such uniformity is achieved by a one-man intake service such as that described by Rapp (1974). Under such a system, where there is one person dealing with and making decisions about all new incoming referrals, there exists a high degree of uniformity of response about such matters as what cases are taken on by social services, what kind of help is offered, and what cases are referred to other agencies. Rapp sees one of the advantages of such a one-man system as being to give a full and realistic view of the work coming into the team, the kinds of demands being made, and the different means which can be found to deal with different cases.

While very few areas today would favour or find it possible to function effectively with what is, in effect, one permanent duty officer, the same advantages of consistency of response and building up an overview of the problems being presented can accrue to an intake team. Such teams are in a position to monitor the demands and needs being expressed and the provisions that are available. The concentration of a small number of workers at intake increases the possibility of consistent and accurate monitoring, and consequently the ready availability of this information can be used to inform central management about policy and planning issues, the areas of shortfall of provision, the needs of particular areas or client groups, and other such matters. Gaining an overview of the needs of the area is important not only for planning and policy decisions but also for the recruitment and deployment of staff within the area.

For example, if there are a large proportion of referrals that require one-off interviews or short-term work, then this indicates that perhaps the size of the intake team needs to be increased to be better able to undertake this work; on the other hand it may be that many referrals are for children at risk or for very vulnerable elderly, needing a long-term commitment from the area, in which case the availability of long-term workers becomes the central issue. Alternatively, it may become evident that a high proportion of referrals are from a particular set of streets, or a specific estate, which may indicate that it would be appropriate for a group of workers to concentrate some effort in this area; such a group would perhaps include workers from the long-term team within whose boundaries the target area is, or some from an outside agency.

Individual intake workers soon pick up a general feeling about what the prevailing needs are and where the areas of highest stress lie. However, there is a tendency for individual workers to be primarily concerned with individual cases. The person who, perhaps, is in the prime position to gain an overview of these matters is the intake senior social worker who will be acquainted with nearly all the incoming work, the source of referral, and the outcome of the referral. As such, it may be that innovatory responses can be developed. Sainsbury and Nixon (1979), for example, in a study of the content of family social work undertaken by the local authority social services department, the probation service, and the local Family Service Unit, found that the health services emerged as the major sources of referral, especially to the social services department. However, although most clients were in contact with the income maintenance and employment services, these were not mentioned as sources of referral.

Social workers may therefore need to pay more attention to income maintenance and employment services and clarify what help can be offered, so that realistic social work help can be considered at an earlier, and perhaps preventive, stage. The intake senior is thus in a position to have a broad overview of incoming work and how it is dealt with and is hence the person who can promote some degree of consistency of service to clients, by deciding with the intake workers where the priorities of the team lie and what is considered the work of the team. The group cohesion and team ethos usually found in intake teams serves to enhance this consistency of response.

One of the advantages to accrue from the establishment of intake teams was a more consistent and uniform service to the public. Intake teams have, however, been criticized for offering a uniform service at the expense of a sympathetic service, and it has been suggested that they devise standardized solutions to problems, or categorize clients into client group or type of problem and then offer a 'pre-packed' solution. Critics believe that intake teams offer a mechanized, impersonal service and, in the name of efficiency and consistency, militate against caring and innovatory responses. While there may at times be elements of truth in these criticisms, features such as those attributed above to intake teams are not inherent components of intake-team organization and are, perhaps, most likely to be evident when intake workers are under considerable pressure, unsure of their role, and unclear about the team's expectations of them or the priorities of the team. That is, they are defensive stances taken by workers under stress. The more supportive the team is, and the more at ease the individual worker feels in his role, the less likely it is that such defensive reactions will take precedence.

While a totally uniform service would be neither possible nor desirable – since it would minimize flexibility and render the service available to clients rigid and mechanistic – there is a need for intake teams to at least consider their collective responses to certain issues, particularly those affecting the provision of a specific service, or financial assistance. Remembering that there are very few demands that cannot be turned away from a social services area team and that referrals of this nature probably constitute only the minority of referrals dealt with by intake workers, there is a vast range of discretion open to the intake worker. When this area of discretion is considered in the light of the gatekeeper role played by intake workers, the power that can be wielded by such individuals is evident. The importance of such discretionary powers is highlighted by, although not exclusive to, the daily decisions made by intake workers to offer or withhold help when faced with a request for a specific service or material help. There are usually general criteria for requests made for a specific service as to who is eligible for such a service, and constraints are imposed by the availability of the service, priorities being established not in terms of need alone but also by availability.

Intake workers are, therefore, able to consider their response in relation to these factors. A more contentious area is in the provision of financial help, whether from the department under Section 1 of the Children and Young Persons Act 1963, or by applying to charities for grants. Shaw (1979), in an article recounting his impressions on returning to work in an intake team after twenty years out of fieldwork, has various interesting comments to make in this area. He found that social workers today, in large post-Seebohm-reorganization departments, seem to have much greater freedom of action and discretion than they had previously, with less scrutiny by senior management. Also, social workers had at their disposal an increased range of resources, albeit matched by the increase in demand and expectations. As regards the use of Section 1 money, he felt that legislation which had been designed to promote family welfare had degenerated into an inefficient means of bailing out an inadequate and rigid social security system.

Social services departments are not primarily in the business of giving financial assistance to individuals and families. However, intake workers are often faced with clients whose problems are basically financial, and the resolution of which requires financial help. In such cases whether or not the client is even considered for assistance rests wholly on the intake worker's discretion. The following example is common of the type presented to intake workers. Mr and Mrs Brent have three children aged ten, five, and two years and Mrs Brent is expecting their fourth child in three months' time. Mr Brent is out of work and receiving unemployment and supplementary benefit. The family's electricity has been disconnected, with arrears standing at £202. The flat is all-electric, the Department of Health and Social Security are not prepared to help, and the electricity board will not reconnect the supply until the full amount of the arrears are paid plus a reconnection fee and a deposit against future bills. There are a range of responses open to the social worker. He may consider that he has little part to play in negotiating and arranging the reconnection of fuel supplies, and so sends the family away, perhaps with the loan of a camping gas cooker so at least they can cook. He may decide to look closely at Mr Brent's financial situation: what benefits he is or should be claiming and what benefits he perhaps could have claimed when he was working so that his arrears would never have accrued, resulting in the disconnection. Mr Brent at least then knows what he is entitled to and if he gets his electricity reconnected eventually may be able to pay his bills in future. Thirdly, the social worker might consider approaching charities for contributions towards the arrears, in an attempt to get the supply reconnected. Finally, the arrears could be paid in part or in full by a grant from Section 1. Which of these responses is selected depends on the discretion of the individual social worker, and his principles and preferences as regards this area of work. Some workers do not hold with Section 1 payments on principle, maintaining that financial support is not a social work function; others may be particularly averse to spending considerable time and effort finding charities prepared to help and balancing their offers and conditions against each other until the full amount required is arrived at.

The individual worker is, therefore, in a position to make a decision about giving or withholding financial help; a decision which all too often bears little relation to any kind of professional social work decision about case management, for the case is not an active one where ongoing work is being undertaken, and the specific request is for financial help. Whilst the causes of the problem may be relevant to what action is taken, such a decision tends to be based primarily on the effect a decision to take no action is likely to have on, usually, the welfare of the children. A more 'deserving' case is more likely to be viewed favourably and hence financial help is more likely to be forthcoming than where no apparent cause for the debt can be found. However, even in the latter case, if there is a very real possibility of the children being received into care, the intake worker may elect to offer help. Consequently, the problems likely to result from no assistance being given play a large part in any decision.

In a long-term case such decisions are more easily arrived at, more information is available, and the financial problem often only one feature of a much wider set of circumstances the social worker is concerned with. In intake, however, the picture is often neither clear nor previously known and the financial difficulties are a factor in their own right and not a symptom of other difficulties. The intake worker, therefore, has to make a decision as to when it is appropriate to consider offering financial help. The question is how rationally and equably such responses are arrived at. If there has been a recent crisis in the family – for example illness, bereavement, or family breakdown – then it is more likely that help will be forthcoming, as the case is likely to be viewed as 'deserving' by charities and social workers are often, perhaps unwittingly, drawn into using such differentiations as 'deserving' and 'undeserving'. Another factor likely to play a part in such decision making is the extent to which the client is prepared to go to press his case. For example, the family that go away quietly when told that social services cannot help financially are less likely to receive help than the family who, perhaps, threaten to leave their children, or whose children are considered 'at risk'.

This is clearly an extremely complex area, and there may well be perfectly valid casework reasons why the last two families require help but the first does not. Perhaps the worrying thing about this area of discretion in financial assistance is that while social workers are often highly critical of supplementary-benefit staff for their abuse of their wide powers of discretion, at least there is an appeals procedure – however lengthy and cumbersome – and tribunal hearings are a right; decisions can be reversed. Social-services clients have no such rights.

Although Shaw (1979) considers that social workers today have greater freedom of action and their work is less scrutinized by senior management than was the case before the Seebohm reorganization, there still tends to be differentiation between 'yes' and 'no' decisions. Intake workers spent a substantial part of their working day turning down requests for services, either because the client has presented at the wrong agency and needs to be referred, or the client is not eligible for a particular service, or the service is not appropriate to the client's needs, or – although eligible and appropriate – the service is not available owing to a shortage of resources. Intake workers are constantly left to make 'no' decisions, either using only their own judgement or in interpreting departmental policy, and to relay such decisions to clients. Intake workers are, therefore, constantly performing their gatekeeping function and turning down requests for service or referring them elsewhere, with relatively little support from their senior colleagues. Where a request is accepted, however – whether it be to help with a bill, receive children into care, place an elderly person in a residential home, or take on a family or individual for casework help – this decision invariably requires consultation and hierarchical sanction.

Intake workers are hence left to interpret confusing policies and procedures and yet try to give an equable service to clients, and detailed consultation probably occurs only where there is a possibility of positive action. Because of the position of intake teams as gatekeepers of resources and services, and their role at the grass roots of the departmental structure, they have considerable potential power to decide operational policy. If individual workers take decisions and base their actions solely on their own judgements they are less likely to have any effect on operational policy than if they act as a team with clear priorities and a reasoned and shared approach to the acceptance or rejection of cases. Where intake teams are able to offer a continuity of reponse in accordance with rationally derived and explicitly stated priorities, the service they offer is likely to be consistent without being rigid.

Parallels between intake workers and general practitioners as front-line practitioners

Intake workers in a social services department can be seen to occupy a similar structural position to general practitioners in the National Health Service. Both are the front-line members of the organization of which they are a part and as such share many problems, and have similar needs in the breadth of their training, knowledge, and skills. Intake workers and general practitioners are faced with working with limited resources which are invariably lacking behind the level of public demand. Both face a similar situation in reception facilities, in that the receptionist plays a critical role in facilitating or hindering the client or patient in making contact with the social worker or doctor. The protective functions played by receptionists are probably more noticeable in general practice where the patient may have to give a series of personal details to the receptionist before being seen by the doctor, and where some requests – particularly for repeat prescriptions – are handled solely by the receptionist, who consults the doctor on the patient's behalf.

General practitioners, like intake workers, are faced with heavy bombardment with demands by the public and an appreciable number of such demands are inappropriate to the agency approached. Likewise, the range of problems faced by general practitioners and intake workers is vast and can vary from the apparently trivial to matters of the utmost gravity – for doctors of life and death, the equivalent for intake workers probably being the deprivation of an individual's liberty.

The general practitioner is the gatekeeper of the Health Services in much the same way that the intake worker can be viewed as the gatekeeper of the social services department and of the services of other agencies. The general practitioner, like the intake worker, is the initial contact for those trying to obtain some form of help or service. Both, therefore, are interested primarily in the problem the patient or client is presenting and the history leading up to that presentation. Having established the nature of the problem, a decision then has to be made about how to deal with it. Sometimes, in both settings, one contact is sufficient and the matter is resolved, the patient or client being advised to re-refer when problems arise. Alternatively the general practitioner or intake worker may decide that they can treat the problem with their own resources but will need to see the patient or client again, either at the agency or on a home visit. It may, however, be the case that the general practitioner feels he cannot treat the patient alone but needs the help of others to aid him in his diagnosis. He may then refer the patient to hospital, for instance for an X-ray or pathology test. Such tests then assist the doctor in making a diagnosis.

For the intake worker similar instances arise. For example, an intake worker may be dealing with a complex family problem including marital difficulties and consequent disturbed behaviour on the part of the children, and the family may also be having protracted difficulties in claiming benefit. The intake worker, while retaining overall responsibility for the case, might enlist the assistance of a local advice agency or Claimants Union in advising on how best to resolve the benefit problem. Having established where the problem lies in claiming benefit the worker is in a better position to assess the family's capabilities and how they cope with such problems, hence building a more complete picture of the family's functioning.

The general practitioner may decide in other cases that he or she is either unable to make a diagnosis, or else he or she requires confirmation of the diagnosis already made and possibly further specialist treatment such as is likely to be available only from a consultant in that particular field. The general practitioner may then refer the patient to be seen for an opinion or seen and treated by a particular consultant.

This is somewhat akin to the intake worker deciding a client requires long-term help and transferring the case to a long-term worker. This latter may or may not be a specialist in that particular field of work, depending on the organizational structure of the department and the deployment of staff between specialist and generic roles. Specialist advisers in social services departments tend to be hierarchically superior to fieldworkers and to be centrally based, advising social workers on various matters but not necessarily having direct contact with the client, unlike hospital consultants who usually advise only after seeing the patient. In both general practice and intake work there are occasions when the patient or client is admitted to residential care, usually hospital for a patient and a variety of resources, depending on the age and nature of the problem, for clients. In both cases the doctor or social worker retains a certain interest but the caring is done by others. However, in this area the social worker probably has somewhat more control over the course of events once a client is 'in care' – whether it be in a foster home, children's home, hostel, or residential home for the elderly – than the general practitioner has once the patient is in hospital, for at this point the hospital team take full control of the care of the patient.

There are, therefore, significant similarities between the practice of general practitioners and that of intake workers. Both offer a primarily problem-focused service to the general public, with few prerequisites as to whether an individual is eligible for service. In the case of the general practitioner the patient usually needs to be on his or her list, in the case of intake worker to live in the relevant catchment area. This gives the general practitioner a small advantage over the intake worker of having some degree of selectivity in the patients accepted, along with the ultimate sanction of taking an individual off his or her list. However, such considerations do not affect the bulk of the work undertaken. Both services function on the basis of patient or client demand, leaving the responsibility basically with the individual to seek help, with very little, if any, regular checking up. Both the general practitioner and the intake worker are faced with a wide diversity of cases and hence both need a very wide range of knowledge and skills to determine the most appropriate course to be taken with a particular patient or client.

It can be said equally of the general practitioner and the intake worker that they are a Jack-of-all-trades. In both cases this does not preclude a particular interest in a specialist area and a certain amount of professional practice in this area of work, but it highlights the overriding need for a broad basis in training and experience across a range of specialist skills, knowledge, and expertise. It can be argued, therefore, that general practice is a medical specialism in its own right on the basis of the type and structural location of work it undertakes, although it is as much removed from the traditional medical specialisms such as surgery, psychiatry, gynaecology, and neurology as intake work is from the traditional specialisms of child care, mental welfare, and welfare work.

What in the field of medicine is known as diagnosis is known in social work practice as assessment. Diagnosis or assessment are the hallmarks of the work of the general practitioner or intake worker. Younghusband states: 'professional social work deserves credit for making assessment (social diagnosis) a fundamental of practice and devoting much effort to refining this in the light of new knowledge' (Younghusband 1978a: 24). Assessment constitutes an essential part of intake work as does diagnosis in medicine.

However, there is little point in the general practitioner diagnosing that Mrs B is suffering from anaemia unless he goes on to treat the condition and if it seems likely to recur addresses himself to the cause of the problem and whether this can be rectified. Likewise in social work, assessment is all very fine but must be viewed as a means to an end, not as an end in itself. Neither patients nor clients usually visit the doctor or social worker just to have their condition diagnosed or problem assessed. They want, and legitimately expect, to be helped. Diagnostic and assessment activities are, therefore, justifiable only if they contribute to effective intervention. Just as doctors are not paid to carry out lengthy and expensive series of tests solely for their own enjoyment with no positive outcome for the patient, social workers are not paid to write clients' biographies or delve into the subtleties of their psychosexual functioning unless they can show that such activities increase their effectiveness in helping the client. The hallmark of current social work practice, the case conference, has been criticized for comprising fifty-eight minutes of discussing the history of the case and the factors causing the current situation and only two minutes of attempts to establish definite plans for the future.

Loewenstein (1974) defines the main activities of an intake team to be assessment activities, including making assessments or en-quiries before the allocation of a case or on behalf of other depart-ments; and helping activities, including liaising with other agencies and giving advice, information, and support. As a major activity of an intake worker it is, therefore, important that assessments are carefully carried out and comprehensively presented. Haphazard assessments, like wrong diagnoses, can have dire consequences, and lack of assessment, like lack of diagnosis, can cause a situation to grow out of hand to the point where it is virtually untreatable, whereas if diagnosed early and treated accordingly it may have been overcome. Consequently professionals in any field located at a point within their organization where they are in a position to pinpoint difficulties at an early stage before they grow out of manageable proportion have a duty to thoroughly diagnose or assess such problems and decide on the relevant course of action, for such action may carry considerable preventive potential.

The aim of an assessment is to answer a series of questions designed to give a measure of the magnitude of the problem, knowledge of which is essential for planning and implementing a successful strategy of intervention. Indicators of the magnitude and severity of a problem are given by such factors as the pervasiveness of the problem; the degree of impairment or disablement associated with it; the persistence of the problem and whether it is chronic, bearing in mind that a high proportion of 'acute' problems improve in a short time irrespective of what practitioners do; and the prognosis of the problem.

Assessments that follow these lines give a sound basis upon which to plan social work intervention and decide what sort of intervention is likely to be most appropriate. It would, for example, indicate which cases may be appropriately dealt with on a short-term basis in intake and which are more likely to require long-term intervention.

Such predictions are not always borne out by the subsequent course of the case but at least form a basis from which to begin and give some indication as to the likely developments. Adequate diagnosis in medical practice and adequate assessment in social work, therefore, enables the practitioner to take the necessary next steps in dealing with the problem in terms of deciding whether or not to refer the problem elsewhere – to a different agency or a specialist within the same organization – when to refer it, and to whom. General practitioners and intake workers need to quickly build up their skills in rapid and accurate diagnosis or assessment so that the patient or client receives appropriate and effective help. The importance of diagnosis or assessment and the difficulties caused when they are not competently carried out, along with the breadth of knowledge, skill, and experience required to fulfil the task effectively, suggest that general practice and intake work are similar in that they are specialist areas of work requiring highly qualified and experienced practitioners.

It has been suggested that since the model of general practice and the expectations of general practitioners are well established in the public mind, social services departments may be well advised to follow a similar mode of organization at intake level. Oriss (1974) suggests that in setting up an intake team the model of the general practitioner's surgery should be used, with specific opening times and an appointments system. This, he argues, is comprehensible to clients who are already familiar with such a mode of organization from their experience of general practice, and also serves as a means of rationing the service offered. Whilst there are clear organizational and administrative advantages in such a model, it militates against the objectives of both physical and psychological accessibility espoused by the Seebohm Report and seen to be one of the great advantages of area team organization, by which area teams become a more functional part of the community that they serve. Such a model also encourages clients' expectations of social workers to be similar to their expectations of a general practitioner. That is, the client will go to the social worker, describe the problem, and the social worker will then give an answer to the problem, whether it be a solution, advice, or 'treatment'.

However, the major difference between general practice and social services intake lies in this area: whereas in the medical model of practice the doctor is assumed to possess a body of knowledge unavailable to the patient, and, therefore, to prescribe for the patient, who is usually expected to take a passive role in the proceedings and accept what the doctor offers, in the social work model the client is viewed as an interacting element in the problem presented and is consequently expected to take a more active part in working towards a resolution of the problem. This difference in approach can result in discrepant expectations between worker and client and subsequent misunderstanding and miscommunication. It is thus important that expectations are shared and made explicit at an early stage, both client and worker being clear about their roles and how work is to be undertaken. There are, therefore, significant similarities between the role of the general practitioner and intake worker as front-line workers concerned with initial diagnosis and assessment of problems presented to them and making critical decisions on how to most effectively deal with these problems, including whether or not to refer elsewhere, if so where, and the inevitable frustrations caused by shortages in resources.

The difference lies in the style of work with the individual patient or client and the mutual expectations of this encounter. Social workers and general practitioners, often at loggerheads and equally scathing about each others' shortcomings, share more common frustrations and difficulties in their day-to-day work than they often realize. Both are dealing with problems that are either of an acute or short-term nature and amenable to some relatively limited form of intervention, and with chronic problems which are not amenable to any consistent management. Complex and long-term difficulties are usually transferred to the relevant specialist. Medical practice, being symptom-orientated, passes the patient between different specialists for different complaints. For example, a patient with a chronic neurological disorder who then develops a non-related skin condition will be treated for the latter by a different specialist. In long-term social work, as a result of the move towards genericism, any social problems that develop within the family will be the province of the one social worker, who may nevertheless seek specialist advice from elsewhere, although long-term workers do tend to shape their case loads with a bias towards those areas of work which they find most interesting. The general practitioner and the intake worker, on the other hand, are both generic practitioners of the first order by virtue of their location in their respective organizations, and hence require an extremely broad range of knowledge, skills, and information to work effectively.

Responses to pressure in intake teams

The intake worker is in a key position to determine whether or not a client's needs or demands are met. He may either facilitate or obstruct the client's passage through the welfare maze. Barnes (1975), in arguing for greater community participation by social services departments so that community-based workers are in an important position to transmit community feeling to policy makers, describes the duty officer/intake worker as a 'flak catcher'. That is, he sees the duty officer as constantly prevaricating when faced by a request, being unable to make any decision without referring to those higher in the hierarchy. Placing such a person at the point of initial contact, he argues, ensures minimum cost in the resources of the agency because clients, having called once, simply do not call back. Although this is something of a caricature – perhaps more applicable to duty-rota systems just after the Seebohm reorganiz-ation where the duty officer often had virtually no commitment to seeing new clients on duty and where the main aim was often to take the bare minimum of details and send the client off with the gesture 'Someone will look into it and be in touch' – it seems to highlight the powerful position the duty officer is in.

If the agency's objective is to provide an effective service to clients then it is important that the organization and support of the intake workers is carefully considered, and efforts made to minimize negative responses. Intake workers, because of their structural position in the organization and the wide range of work viewed by the public and other professionals as being the province of the social services department, are faced with an immensely wide range of needs, demands, and enquiries. They are required to fill a wide variety of roles, and assess a multitude of situations to ascertain what is required, ranging from assessing a client's financial eligibility for a particular service to offering a casework service to, for example, a recently widowed mother. The breadth of the duties required of them often leads to tension and conflict between competing demands on their time, skill, and expertise. Along with this, there is the constant pressure of lack of adequate resources, as the background against which the intake worker has to function and which he has to convey to clients. As Prodgers says:

'Despite the high blown idealism of Seebohm, social services departments have never had the resources to fully meet client need . . . social workers are constantly in a situation where, trained to provide an effective professional service to the client, they are unable to because of bureaucratic/administrative structures.'

(Prodgers 1979: 12)

There is, therefore, an inherent contradiction in the intake workers' position; they are personally motivated and professionally trained to offer a service, but are unable to do so because of the lack of resources of the agency. The intake worker, therefore, has to mediate within himself between his personal response and that of the agency. Since intake workers are in the business of saying no and explaining why clients needs cannot be met they are in a vulnerable position, constantly faced by client need but often unable to meet it. To overcome their own distaste for this and to assuage their personal feelings of guilt about the lack of resources, their response is often couched in terms such as: 'I would like to help you, but agency policy forbids me'. They thereby externalize agency policy and blame this, absolving themselves from personal responsibility for the decision. Another commonly used means of absolving the individual intake worker from refusing a request is to tell the client that it will be discussed with a senior – that is, implying to the client that it will be another person in the hierarchy who makes the decision.

Intake workers as individuals and groups, therefore, develop strategies to help resolve the conflicts of being a professional worker at the interface of a large organization and the public at large. The basic conflict for the intake worker is having to say 'no', and this is also a prerequisite for intake workers who need to be able to refuse clients' demands to protect themselves, fellow intake workers, long-term teams, and the department itself from being overwhelmed by the demands being made upon it. Social workers are caught between seeking professional, innovative solutions and bureaucratic, ritualistic ones, ending up by adopting a utilitarian stance. As Prodgers concludes: 'Lack of resources compelled the agency to take a defensive, inward looking approach to client need and the intake worker becomes a tool in this process' (Prodgers 1979: 14).

One of the major sources of stress for intake workers results from inappropriate referrals from other agencies who have little or no understanding of what social services are able to offer. Interestingly, in social services departments the front-line workers are much more highly trained than in other agencies – for example, housing and social security – and may, therefore, be expected to take a more professional and responsible attitude towards clients. However, it seems likely that other agencies often suggest clients go along to social services as a strategy to placate an angry or distressed client. However, having been advised to call by the initial agency the client, not unreasonably, builds up the expectation that the social services department will be able to do something to resolve the problem.

It is, therefore, not uncommon for a client to arrive at the social services department and ask to see a social worker as they have been sent by the housing department about, for example, their over-crowding. There is nothing the intake worker is likely to be able to suggest or advise, but the client is now understandably irate at having been sent on a fool's errand, and time has to be spent in at least trying to explain to and placate the client, and in complaining to the housing department for the inappropriateness of their referral. Likewise, especially when under pressure, social security are prone to refer to social services individuals who initially present at the Department of Health and Social Security saying they have no money. Unless the client has a clear understanding of agency function and is prepared to do battle with social security, they are likely to present at intake after apparently wasted hours only to be advised that they are at the wrong place, and social services is not an income-maintenance agency. As a result of such a mis-referral the intake worker, to avoid sending the angry and frustrated client on a further wild good chase, begins protracted negotiations on the client's behalf.

Often when intake teams were first being established there was a considerable concern expressed as to whether individual workers would be able to withstand the pressure such work entailed. Corrie (1976) in her survey questioned whether intake workers received emotional satisfaction from the type of work dealt with by intake teams. Just under 50 per cent said they did, approximately 30 per cent were ambivalent, and the remainder either did not find any emotional satisfaction or did not know whether they did or not. The frustrations encountered were found to be similar irrespective of area: lack of adequate staffing ratios in both intake and long-term teams, falling standards because of pressure and lack of time, lack of resources, frustrations with bureaucracy, and frustration in not seeing a case through when it is transferred to long-term. When asked whether 'personality factors' were seen as important in the selection of intake workers, an overwhelming 78 per cent replied in the affirmative. This suggests that intake work is to a certain extent different in nature to long-term work. The inherent tension in the intake structure – that is, from having to refuse services on the basis of lack of resources rather than any assessment of client need – tends over time to militate against the intake worker's ability to respond with sensitive understanding and warmth and towards an attitude of increased formalism, rigidity, and insensitivity.

Case-management decisions may come to be made on the basis of administrative rather than professional social work criteria. When workers become so restricted in their ability to offer what they feel to be a meaningful service by the lack of resources available to them, there is the danger that administrative efficiency may replace social work practice as the major source of job satisfaction.

As has been previously discussed (see Chapter 3) informal groups play an important role in helping individuals cope with pressure and stress, evolving group norms to cope with stress and sometimes sanctioning defensive reactions on the part of members. Intake teams generally present as very cohesive groups, members needing to feel that there are others who understand their position and can be called on in times of crisis. Team work and team cohesion are generally acknowledged as highly important in intake teams as a means of helping individual members cope with the pressures to which the job subjects them. Whilst such group support is clearly of great value, the other side of the coin is the control and pressure that groups generally exert to ensure members conform to group norms. This can have either positive or negative effects. Where an intake team is well established with high professional standards, a general commitment to free and open communication, flexibility of practice, and keenness to look at new ways of working, conformity to such norms would be seen as a positive advantage of such group pressure and control. On the other hand, an intake team which is not functioning well, is priding itself on getting through the work but is giving little actual help to clients, dealing with most work on a one-off basis or by referring it elsewhere whenever this is possible, will likewise instil these norms into members and such group pressure and control may well be viewed negatively.

An individual worker's response can be influenced by what Shaw (1979) calls the 'fantasy team in the head'. This is particularly the case for new workers and those who lack confidence in their own practice and decision making. In intake teams there is a much higher degree of sharing between members in discussion about cases and in decision making than is generally the case in long-term teams. The individual worker is, therefore, that much more accountable to the team, and his responses to clients may well be influenced as much by the need to conform to the group norms as by the client's needs. The individual worker's practice is, therefore, dictated to a significant extent by the need to be seen to have done a 'good' interview, not been too soft, too hard, or whatever the current group norms dictate. For example, an intake worker in a team which prides itself on rarely giving out money under Section 1 of the Children and Young Persons Act 1963, feeling that the statutory income maintenance agencies should be encouraged to fulfil their obligations, will be less likely to suggest such a payment to a family in acute financial difficulties, even where the individual worker feels this may be appropriate, than in a team where such payments are often made in a wide variety of situations.

Spencer (1973), in discussing the various support mechanisms social services organizations have developed to help their staff, considers the work team, along with the supervisory and consultative machinery, to be the most important. The work group acts as a powerful force in influencing and controlling the behaviour of its members and may have either a positive or a negative effect on service to clients depending on whether it encourages innovation or supports defensive stances taken by members. Spencer goes on to say: 'The principles of supervision and consultation are probably even more important than the work team from the angle of support provision' (Spencer 1973: 7). The individual worker, therefore, has two sources to look to for support, his team and his supervising senior. The intake senior social worker, therefore, is in a key position to influence the norms and goals of his team members and to encourage individuals to consider more innovative ways of working, and thereby to shape the ethos of the team.

Adequate support requires not only that there are adequate and appropriate personnel in supervisory/consultative positions, but also that they are readily available to their team members. There is little support a team can derive from an intake senior if he has numerous other responsibilities which mean he is often either out of the office or, if there, not available to team members. Support, as Spencer points out, is not a goal in itself but a means by which to facilitate work with clients. If support comes to be seen as an end in itself there is the risk that the team will succumb to ideological conformity, self-validating belief systems, and charismatic leadership.

Intake teams were originally set up as a pragmatic, organizational response to the situation in which social services departments found themselves after the Seebohm reorganization. Whilst many believe that they are the most effective way of dealing with the intake process, because intake teams have demonstrated that they can cope with an increasing number of referrals with no concomitant increase in resources, it can also be suggested that they are a means of containing problems, benefiting the agency rather than the client. Whereas one of the objectives behind the setting up of intake teams was the better matching of needs to resources, paradoxically they may have had the opposite effect by protecting the agency from the impact of client demands rather than helping meet community needs. As Jones points out: 'An intake group can find itself serving administrative needs rather than those of its clients, because it falls to the group to explain just why the social services department is unable to match its exiguous resources to the needs it uncovers' (Jones 1974: 67).

Another of the theoretical strands in the establishment of intake teams was the development of an efficient, sympathetic, and uniform service. Prodgers (1979) points to the need to be alert to the danger that the aim of providing a uniform service may lead to the development of standardized solutions and set ways of dealing with problems that may not be the most appropriate in all cases. Similarly, the desire for uniformity may lead to rigidity and so militate against a sympathetic service. The style of work in intake teams is different from that in other settings, partly due to the pace of the work but also because intake workers tend to be more closely attached to the administration of the services than workers in other settings. Consequently, as Boucher notes:

> 'the idea of intake is rooted in the organization of the agency rather than directly in the needs of the public, the worker's perception of his role within the agency changes and the loyalty to the agency itself and to colleagues becomes more important.'

(Boucher 1976: 13)

There is, however, no inherent reason why – as long as intake workers are alert to these dilemmas – social work practice and hence the service offered to individual clients by intake teams should suffer, and there is much to suggest that clients are afforded a more efficient, effective, and rapid response by intake teams than by other means of dealing with the intake process.

5

Implications of the intake model

Introduction

The intake model of organization serves to highlight a number of issues that pertain to social services departments as a whole, and to the role, function, and needs of such departments. Because intake teams are front-line operational units for the department it is at this point that departmental policy becomes effected. Intake teams, being the 'one-door' through which virtually all requests for service have to pass, are, therefore, in a position to control the work flow to not only the social services department, but also to other agencies, by being in a position to accept, reject, or refer elsewhere a request for service. Such teams, therefore, perform a gatekeeping function. As a result, they are in a position to determine what, out of the range of demands presented and the diversity of roles intake workers are called upon to play, are appropriate to the department.

However, to be in a position to decide what is and what is not appropriate – and even if appropriate, what will actually be dealt with – there has to be at intake level a mutual and agreed understanding of the system of rationing and priorities to which the team is working. To be of service to the client, even where the client's request is deemed low priority or inappropriate to the department, the intake worker needs a vast range of information at his disposal on such disparate areas as departmental policies, legislation, welfare rights, the role of voluntary agencies and what work they undertake, developments in professional social work thinking, and much more besides. Therefore, because of the extremely powerful position of intake workers, they need to have an understanding of, and working relationship with, other local resources to be in the best position to help and advise clients as only one of a network of agencies within the community.

The gatekeeper role of intake teams

Intake teams cannot be considered in isolation from the rest of the area team, the department as a whole, and other agencies in the area, because they are functionally related to all of these. Intake teams play a major role as the gatekeeper for both the statutory services and other agencies; they are in the crucial position of deciding who gets what service. The intake worker functions not only in his own area and department but also in handling referrals to other agencies in the social work, statutory, and voluntary fields. To function effectively in dealing with other agencies the intake worker needs to build up a reasonably detailed level of knowledge on the role, function, working, and philosophy of other agencies. For example, there is little point in initially sending a client with a landlord-tenant problem to a solicitor when there is a competent and efficient tenancy relations officer attached to a local advice centre. Likewise there is no point in sending an elderly lady to a voluntary organization to ask for a food parcel when that organization accepts referrals only from social services and not direct from clients.

Since the Seebohm reorganization social work has tended to project an image of itself to the public as offering a potential solution to a wide range of personal and social problems, consequently raising expectations that cannot subsequently be met. Requests arising out of these expectations are invariably first presented at the point of intake. The task of the intake worker then becomes one of singling out those problems that either can or ought to be dealt with by the social services department. Hence intake workers tend to classify and categorize cases at the point of referral, which may detract from their arriving at a comprehensive picture of the individual case, but which is often found necessary to make decisions about appropriate allocation of the case – whether it should be handled by short-term work in the intake team, or go direct to a long-term team or to an outside agency. It is, therefore, of great importance to develop clear criteria within the area team as to what the expectations are of types of work undertaken. As Gill and Boaden point out, the intake worker occupies a crucial position and the action that he takes is vital since: 'intake, because of its crucial position, not only affects the client's passage through the welfare maze but also the ultimate quantity and quality of welfare provision' (Gill and Boaden 1976: 11).

The span of social work activities is now so broad that many problems that are finally either presented by the client or are referred to social services departments are largely insoluble, hence contributing to the public's somewhat blurred image of what social work has to offer. Owing to the vast range of undifferentiated problems that area teams are bombarded with, it is often a major task to make an assessment, decide and plan what action is most appropriate, or what agency would be better able to help. The intake worker is consequently often described as a Jack-of-all-trades, and implicit in this is the suggestion that he is master of none – a debate that will be taken up in the final chapter. Voicing an expression of concern at the excessive range of duties loaded both explicitly and implicitly onto social workers Hankinson, Director of Social Services in Sunderland, commented: 'We're the twentieth century undertakers – undertaking all the dirty jobs that no one else will do'.

It has been suggested that such a wide range of demands as are characteristically presented to intake workers tends to militate against the worker being able to sustain a strong caring motivation, and reduces responses to a much more mechanistic level. However, the intake worker is not wholly at the mercy of incoming referrals. As the gatekeeper for the resources of the department he must: decide whether social work intervention is appropriate; make initial decisions about the availability of resources, both of capital and manpower, to deal with the problem in the light of the area's extant priorities; and control the flow of work through the office. In addition to his role as gatekeeper the intake worker also functions as educator and publicity agent in dealing with new clients. All these are powerful roles for encouraging or discouraging clients and potential clients from contacting the department, and hence can be used to expand or contract the flow of work to the agency. Intake workers, can, therefore, be viewed as being at the whim of an uncontrolled bombardment with referrals, but at the same time can use their power as gatekeeper to, either consciously or unconsciously, control the flow of work to themselves and hence to the whole department. Goldberg and Fruin (1976) suggest that with the mushrooming of social services departments social workers may undertake less direct service delivery and counselling contact but rather function as managers, allocating resources and working as enablers to social work assistants, volunteers, and neighbourhood groups. Whether or not this is the case, it serves to highlight and formalize the crucial role now played, usually implicitly, by intake workers in relation to resource allocation.

The structure and ethos of the organization within which social work is a major activity is likely to have a profound effect on the nature of social work practice within that organization. In local authority social services departments a generalist perspective is usually the prevalent one, supervisory and management skills covering a wide diversity of areas of work being those that are rewarded. Within area teams intake tends to be the most generalist area of work, so as to be able to cope effectively with the wide range of demands made on the team. With the amalgamation in 1971 of the previously distinct and more specialized departments into the unified social services departments, and the emergence of the generic social worker, much specialist expertise and knowledge was lost. This was compensated for in some degree by the voluntary sector. Younghusband (1978a) points out that by the mid-1970s a great and increasing amount of voluntary effort existed both locally and nationally to provide general co-ordination of specific services for particular groups of people. One of the functions of these voluntary organizations has been to provide specialist services as a part of the resources available to social workers.

There has also, over the past decade, been a tremendous growth in the development of information and advice agencies, funded both by local authorities and voluntary bodies and catering for either specific groups, for example young people or people with housing problems, or as more general advice centres, along the lines of the well-established Citizens Advice Bureaux. Consequently, social services departments are just one of a number of agencies which together form a network of 'helping' agencies. Most have their own particular specialism but function across a broader range of problems. Social services departments, being a statutory agency and relatively well established, are often the first agency to be approached. Goldberg *et al.* (1977), in studying one year's intake of cases to an area office in Southampton, found that the social services department seemed to be being increasingly used as an information and advice centre and as a referral agency, especially for financial problems.

Similarly, Day *et al.* (1978), reviewing 100 cases presented to an area team, found that although nearly half the department's time was spent in work with families a considerable amount of staff time was used in dealing with queries which staff thought should not have been presented to them and could have been equally well dealt with by the Citizens Advice Bureau. The question then arises as to why these clients were not referred to a more appropriate agency, since this is always an option open to the intake worker, providing there is such an agency in the area. This example highlights the necessity for clear thinking on behalf of the whole area team but particularly by the intake team as to what its brief is, what work the team is set up to undertake, and what the priorities of the team are in the inevitable decisions that have to be made in the context of limited and usually inadequate resources. Such guidelines at departmental level are necessarily broad and general; the real power lies with the individual who is taking the decisions on each case.

If there is no open communication in the intake team in an honest endeavour to reach some operational guidelines about the task of the team, individual workers are left to decide for themselves what is and is not appropriate work for the team. They may consequently find themselves, as in the team mentioned above, undertaking work they do not feel they should be dealing with and which another, available, agency could handle equally well. Such matters as this are ones that need examination and decision on a team basis in the light of the team's priorities.

Intake workers, therefore, occupy a critical role as gatekeepers to the services and resources of their own agency and to a range of other agencies. They are in a position to either facilitate or obstruct the client from receiving such diverse services as a place in a residential home for their mother, a slot-meter for their electricity, a subsidy for their childminding fees, sessions of family therapy, individual counselling, or a holiday for their handicapped brother. Hence intake teams cannot be viewed in isolation but are closely interwoven in a network of services and agencies in the area served.

The diversity of roles at intake

Cooper (1979) lists the many and varied roles that social workers are called upon to fill: friend, adviser, counsellor, lawyer, advocate, court official, guardian of the rights of children, guardian of the rights of the mentally ill, witness, prosecutor, adoption officer, local government officer, welfare officer, financier, accountant, consoler, confidant, and therapist. In addition, he adds other roles that are not generally listed in the social work literature, such as: fixer, form filler, scapegoat, buck holder, and (increasingly) apologist for services that do not exist. Although to some extent all social workers in whatever setting will be called upon to fill a number of these roles it is at the point of intake that the tremendous diversity of expectations which clients bring to the department is most apparent and consequently it is the intake worker who is most likely to have to change rapidly from role to role in his daily work to meet the demands placed upon him. Some of the roles expected of social workers require aptitude rather than training, others demand professionalism of a very high order to be carried out effectively. The task for the social worker, however, is not just to know the roles and how to fill them – a considerable expectation in itself – but to know when to play which role. It is in this latter area that the skill, expertise, and sensitivity of the worker is at a premium, and here that the hallmark of the successful and effective intake worker lies. He must not only have at his command a vast range of knowledge and skill but also be able to rapidly assess what is appropriate to the given situation.

Wooton (1978) sees money, or rather the lack of it, as the major problem faced by the clients of social services departments. This she holds to be the case even in the indirect sense that those individuals who are better off financially, finding themselves in similar situations, would employ professional assistance. The need, therefore, of social services clients is to know where to apply for that to which they are entitled. Social work thereby becomes the mammoth task of keeping up with all the relevant rules and regulations governing the highly complex system of welfare-state benefits. The social worker, Wooton says, needs to act as a 'mobile encyclopaedia of welfare rights'. If poverty was abolished, she concludes, 'the major part of social workers' functions would almost certainly disappear' (Wooton 1978: 14). Social workers, therefore, fulfil for the poor the parts played by, for example, accountants, lawyers, surveyors, and therapists for the better off. That is, social workers advise their clients in the fields of financial difficulties and income maintenance, as an accountant might; on their legal obligations and duties as a parent or spouse, as a lawyer might; about their building and house maintenance as a surveyor might; and in the area of their emotional difficulties as might be taken to a private therapist. Wooton sees the primary task of social work today as ensuring that the social services function effectively and that benefits and services reach those that are eligible for them. This in itself demands an encyclopaedic knowledge of social services provision and the capacity to match widely varying needs to the facilities that are available.

This view of social work has hitherto tended to be unacceptable to the profession and there has traditionally been something of a division between advisory and service delivery type functions and traditional casework functions. The former have largely been the province of unqualified social workers and social work assistants and the latter of professionally qualified workers. The effect of this distinction has been to view as relatively low status what is seen as fairly straight-forward advisory and service delivery work in comparison with the higher status afforded to casework skills.

More recently, however, Wooton has hailed the role of the middle-man as being so expert a service as to qualify for professional status in its own right, and increasingly advocacy is being acknowledged and accepted as an important part of the social worker's role. This is highlighted at intake, where the worker is often called upon to act as an intermediary between the client and other services. The client often hopes that 'an official' – the social worker – can arrange for certain rules to be bent, or will be more successful in putting pressure on another department to achieve a particular end, or will be able to negotiate on the client's behalf. The unfortunate truth of the matter is that too often the client is right and pressure from the 'official' achieves results whereas the client's representations on his own behalf achieved nothing. Hence the social services department, in the person of the intake worker, has a tendency to undertake innumerable transactions and negotiations that have more to do with expertise in matters of advocacy and negotiation than with traditional social work skills. Furthermore, the fact that the social worker is seen to succeed where the client fails does little for the latter's self-esteem and perpetuates the role of the social worker as middleman.

A few examples may demonstrate the point. One of the most common problems brought to intake workers, which they have no need to deal with, is that of council-house repairs; not in cases so severe that legal action may be contemplated, but where the tap drips, or the window does not shut, or the bath is cracked. Tenants become increasingly frustrated by the lack of action of the main-tenance department despite repeated reporting of the fault and often eventually turn in desperation to social services to see if they can exert pressure to get the repairs done. Another instance is where some Fuel Boards refuse to instal prepayment meters for customers at their request. Consequently, the arrears mount and mount until a crisis arises when disconnection is a real possibility. At this point the Fuel Board will, at the request of the social services department, instal a prepayment meter where possible. By this time the client has arrears and has to enter into some agreement to pay these off as well as pay for current supply through the meter. Some charities will issue grants only through social services – so where, for example, the Citizens Advice Bureau is trying to raise money for a client of theirs towards a fuel bill, social services may well have to operate on a purely administrative, letter-writing basis to request a grant from a particular charity. Some volunteer agencies will not take referrals direct from clients but only from social workers; the client rings the social worker and says: 'I need my hedge cut, I can't do it myself because of my arthritis', and the social worker relays this same message to the volunteer agency. Claimants are much more likely to win appeals at Supplementary Benefits Tribunals when they are represented, particularly by social workers.

All these examples are instances of intake workers being used, either at the request of the client or other agencies, as a middleman or negotiator and where this is the primary function of the worker. Work of this kind occupies a substantial part of an intake worker's time. While it is clearly not traditionally understood as a social work function, the increasing part such work plays, particularly in intake work as it is largely of a one-off or short-term nature, suggests that it is a major area of work now to be included in the tasks undertaken by intake teams.

The development of intake teams cut across the traditional boundaries of social work practice. No longer is it so easy to divide service delivery from casework tasks, for a team specifically designed with a remit to deal with all new incoming and short-term work will inevitably undertake the whole range of work undertaken by a social services department. Intake workers need to be aware of, and to use, not only facts on welfare rights and the availability of and eligibility for services – hitherto the province of social work assistants – but also the wide range of casework skills traditionally the province of the qualified worker. The problems referred at intake often require an extensive knowledge of departmental and other policies and resources, and of the law. The increasing use by the public of social services departments as information and advice centres, dealing with specific requests, coupled with the intake ethos of a problem-focused service dealing primarily with explicit requests, combine to emphasize the hard service delivery end of the social work spectrum, which is highlighted at intake.

However, there remains what Cooper (1978) calls 'personal sorrow', the heart of the social work inheritance – such problems as bereavement, addiction, isolation, marital discord, emotional deprivation, mental illness, and mental and physical handicap – none of which necessarily bear any relation to financial status. These too are the province of the social services department and are problems which are initially referred to intake workers. Consequently, a social worker who acts as a 'mobile encyclopaedia of welfare rights', performs a very useful and valuable function both for clients and the team, constantly using his or her knowledge in advising clients about their rights, and is unlikely to be underemployed. He or she would, however, have severe shortcomings as an effective intake worker given the wide variety of demands made upon such workers who, therefore, need to encompass both hard knowledge and information along with the more traditional casework skills.

The question sometimes posed as to whether the public want services or therapy is a gross oversimplification. Primarily the public want an identifiable body to carry the responsibility for the vulnerable members of the community. Whether this entails providing services to enable individuals to function at what is considered to be an acceptable level in the community, or whether some sort of therapeutic intervention is used to achieve the same end, would appear to be relatively immaterial to the public. For the individual client, likewise, there is no straightforward answer to the question. Some clients are clearly seeking specific services, which may be deemed appropriate or inappropriate by the social worker, or the client may be unsuccessful in their quest as a result of the overall lack of resources. Alternatively, some clients, particularly the most vulnerable, isolated, or emotionally deprived, are seeking from social services not a specific reply but rather the affirmation that they are not completely rejected and cast aside by society and that they do have some degree of dignity and integrity as human beings. Yet others are consciously seeking help for what is to them an intolerable family or marital situation, and this may include both the provision of specific services – for instance, if there is strain as the result of caring for an elderly and confused relative – as well as a more therapeutic sort of help in, for example, working on the marital problems and the role the elderly relative may play as the scapegoat for other problems.

Given the range and diversity of problems that intake workers are faced with and the types of knowledge and skill required of such workers, intake work emerges as a post-Seebohm-reorganization specialist area. Specialization in social work has traditionally been by client group, reflecting previous agency divisions. Research undertaken by Stevenson and Parsloe (Stevenson 1978) showed that even six years after the Seebohm reorganization and the emergence of generic workers, many social workers still do specialize informally to a greater or lesser extent in work with a particular client group. Such specialization arises primarily out of the individual worker's interest in a particular area of work. This shaping of individual case-loads by personal preference for types of work can be accommodated to a certain extent by methods of allocation. It is, therefore, a real possibility in long-term teams where there is a greater degree of flexibility about which worker takes particular cases. In intake teams allocation is of a quite different order and tends to be along the lines of which worker initially dealt with a referral. Because intake workers have to cover a wide range of work there is less chance of their developing a specialist area of work in terms of client group and a caseload biased in favour of this group. This does not, of course, preclude intake workers from developing or maintaining an interest in a particular area of work, although it does reduce the time available to pursue this interest given the demands of the range of incoming work.

As Stevenson (1978) points out, professional interest is only one reason for specialization; another is the relationship between client need and organizational efficiency – that is, how to arrange work so that it is done more effectively. Intake teams have been one of the few innovations after the Seebohm reorganization at team level and can be viewed as constituting a new and specialist area of work. In this context, however, specialization is not by client group, unless 'new referrals' are to be taken as such, but rather by location and style of work. Intake work indeed constitutes generic work *par excellence*, for intake workers deal with the whole spectrum of client groups. Intake has developed into a particular field of social work practice and one which is a specialism in itself, requiring a particular range of knowledge and skill for its success. Given the range of work undertaken by intake workers and the potentially critical nature of clients' first contacts with the agency, it is now generally considered that intake workers should be experienced social workers who are, therefore, able to make more complete and confident initial assessments and work towards the early resolution of problems at a point when there may be greater potential for change.

Workers often start in intake teams with only a vague realization of what such work entails, and their learning 'on the job' entails considerable reorientation of their style of work and knowledge. Intake work clearly demands particular skills and knowledge on the part of social workers and this needs to be clearly recognized for training purposes to better equip intake workers for this area of work.

Rationing and priorities

Social services departments are constantly engaged in rationing and setting priorities at all levels, since resources are scarcely ever adequate to meet needs. Questions of rationing and priorities are not, therefore, the province of the intake process alone but are – or should be – central to the whole department's thinking. However, it is at intake that such issues are highlighted, in terms of acceptance or rejection of client need by the agency. Front-line social workers, particularly intake workers, are in some ways the key policy makers for the department, and a major part of agency policy comprises, in effect, the sum total of individual decisions made by individual social workers at the point of intake.

Departmental guidelines and the legislative framework provide a backdrop against which decisions are made. They are usually, however, of a sufficiently general nature as not to dictate particular responses required of the social worker. There are, of course, some areas of work – notably child abuse – where just such guidelines are laid down and there is no doubt throughout departments, at all levels, of the degree of priority afforded such cases. However, in other areas of work, while individual team members make decisions with little consultation with their colleagues, they inevitably have less effect than where the team as a whole acts on the basis of explicit objectives, and clearly defined criteria and priorities. Where there is no such clarity *ad hoc* responses result which may bear little relation to client need. Other considerations come into play, as Hall points out:

'Frequently, as a result, services are received not by those in "greatest need" (by any definition of the term) but by the most vocal, the most persistent, the most articulate, those best able to understand the ways of bureaucracy, the better educated and so on.'

(Hall 1975: 17)

Rationing itself is, therefore, a fact of life; the crucial question is how this rationing is done. Scott (1974) describes seven common ways of rationing services, most of which can be found in use in social services departments. The most obvious means of rationing is rationing by price, hitherto largely rejected in social services departments, but in times of economic constraint and cutbacks it may well play a part, for example in charges or increased charges for services such as home helps, child minding, day nurseries, adaptations for the handicapped, and disabled parking badges. Price, therefore, does play a part, albeit a minor one, in allocation and rationing by social services at field level.

A second, more insidious, form of rationing commonly found is rationing by delay – both informal, in clients being kept waiting a long time, delay in answering telephone calls, etc., and formal delays by such measures as the generation of waiting lists. In the duty systems prevalent in the early 1970s a waiting period of six to eight weeks from initial request to subsequent action was not uncommon. Waiting lists also exist for specific services such as residential accommodation and day-nursery places.

Barriers to access are another means of rationing and were specifically commented on by the Seebohm Committee, such as offices being difficult to get to and a lack of publicity about services. There can also be direct barriers at the point of application, such as requiring a written referral. Such barriers can become deterrents to prospective applicants, as can such factors as the stigma thought to be attached to seeking help; the poor nature of reception and waiting room facilities; and the unsuitability of many buildings for the elderly, handicapped, and those with children.

Ignorance of how social services departments function and what they do are further deterrents before contact, and even once contact is established deterrents include such matters as complex form filling being required for certain services. The question of eligibility also plays a part in the rationing process by categorizing people as 'in' or 'out' of line for service provision by such factors as age and geographical location. Once contact has been established – that is, once the filtering and initial assessment activities are completed, and the problem clarified, then some decision about future contact has to be made, and rationing once again plays a major role. Especially relevant is the question of what resources, including manpower, the agency has available. Services may be rationed by spreading available resources very thinly across the board – that is, by trying to give some service to all – but the quality of the service is hence likely to be very low. This situation is particularly likely where there is no clear priority setting within the team, which therefore tries to meet all needs in a superficial, *ad hoc* way, paying little heed to the effectiveness of their intervention, with little or no discussion about what areas of work it is felt should be accorded highest priority.

Finally, the personal preference of the worker also plays a part in rationing activities. All workers have their own individual preferences for types of work and feel particularly interested in, or effective with, particular problem areas or client groups. Consequently, a social worker particularly interested in working with families with a mentally ill member is likely to afford such work higher priority than a worker interested primarily in working with adolescents. Therefore, the personal preferences of the worker concerned are highly likely to have an effect on the outcome of applications for help, and hence are a further way of implicitly rationing services.

Many features of these rationing practices are implicit and inconsistent. Rationing is largely inevitable and, therefore, needs to be rational, consistent, and explicit both to agency workers and the general public, and also to other professional colleagues who refer cases, such as GPs and health visitors. The concept of rationing implies the idea of priority setting – once a rationing process becomes explicit, recognized, and operationalized, then a consequent set of priorities has to be decided upon. Such a setting of priorities is necessary not simply as a broad statement of agency policy, but at an operational level as the rationale on which day-to-day decisions are made at grass-roots level. That is, the implementation of rationing and priority-setting decisions rests with the worker at the intake point. It is left largely to fieldworkers at this level to convey to applicants the limitations of service and the reasons for this. A wide range of variables determines such priorities, which may include many disparate elements such as source of referral, degree of internal and external political significance of the problem, type of client problem, the likelihood of adverse publicity for the department, the severity of the problem and degree of vulnerability of the client, the influence of central government policy, the influence of pressure groups, the range of resources external to social services in the area, the prevalence of particular needs, and the skills and abilities within the agency.

The criteria used to determine priorities need to be explicit, otherwise the likelihood is that severe problems will arise in implementation. The effect of loose and woolly criteria is a lack of consistency in response to clients and other agencies, workers interpreting the system individually as they see fit or find that it suits them on a particular occasion. The resulting service is likely to be very uneven.

Hall (1975) has developed an operational priority system as one method by which a team of social workers can define priorities as a basis for decision making at the point of intake. This holds that the decision-making process about priorities includes an extremely complex interplay between the problem itself, however defined, and the response which the agency feels is appropriate; both of these being considered in the light of the incidence of the problem in the community. This system, therefore, acknowledges the tension that is created when a social worker wishes to give what may be considered an appropriate professional response, but is governed by the common lack of resources, especially professional time, with which to respond. It is suggested that teams can chart against the problems presented the minimum adequate response, maximum feasible response, and the incidence of the problem. Once these are charted then problems are ranked either as high priority and thereby receive the maximum feasible response, or low priority when they receive minimum adequate response, such decisions being taken in the light of such considerations as the shortage of resources and the differential incidence of different problems. Such a system formalizes and makes explicit the basis on which many individuals make their own *ad hoc* decisions. As Hall concludes:

> 'In this way the group is clarifying the responses its members might take when problems of that kind crop up at the point of intake. It is not intended to constrain individual workers from making special judgements in the light of the unique circumstances of particular cases, but only to provide guidelines for individual action.'
>
> (Hall 1975: 17)

Whatever decisions are made by a team with the relative priorities accorded to different needs, these must be regularly and systematically reviewed in the light of changing circumstances, such as resource availability and the level of demand. It is, however, clear that the questions of priority setting and rationing are inherently interwoven with an intake team model of organization, and as such must be considered by the team so that there can be a shared and explicit understanding of the priority afforded different areas of work and the reasoning for this.

Information needs of intake workers

Intake workers, to practise efficiently and effectively, need a vast range of information to be easily available to them. The problem of information needs is highlighted at the point of intake owing to the rapid turnover of clients and the diversity of problems presented. Long-term workers, with a fixed caseload, are not usually under the same sort of pressure as intake workers to provide basic information across a wide range of areas. Intake workers, therefore, need readily available sources of information, the content of which can be divided into four main areas.

Since legislation forms the foundation of the work of the department the worker needs a sound grounding in the law, particularly those Acts most commonly in use in day-to-day work such as the various Children's Acts and the Mental Health Act. Copies of the Acts themselves, with the notes of guidance and explanatory material, need to be readily available within the team. However, the bare legislative framework is not sufficient as there are invariably departmental policies on such legislation, and these may vary widely. One classic example is the widely differing facilities made available by different authorities under the Chronically Sick and Disabled Persons Act 1970. The legislative framework alone gives little indication as to what is available in any given authority or how eligibility for services is determined. Basic knowledge and information about the law, therefore, needs to be supplemented by information on departmental policy and procedure; that is, how the authority interprets the law, and how this is then put into effect.

Thirdly, the intake worker needs a vast range of information about resources in the local community, both statutory and voluntary. Such information covers as disparate areas as where local playgroups operate, their opening times, and the name of the organizer, to whether or not there is an optician that will do home visits to the handicapped. As area teams are increasingly being viewed as information and advice centres, the time taken up in dealing with such queries is increasing. It is not a social work task in any real sense to deal with such queries, which can generally be handled by reception staff, but the information is needed by the team to deal with such requests. Finally, intake workers, in common with all social workers, need information about professional social work developments.

In addition to these four areas, there is also the information about the facts that fill out the legal and policy frameworks; for example, it is all very well to know that a client is eligible for a certain social security benefit, but the worker then needs to go further and know how much this is likely to be to establish whether the client is receiving the correct benefit, or would be better off by claiming a different benefit. Likewise, knowing that the authority provides day nurseries for the under fives is of little use unless the worker is also aware of the criteria used to assess eligibility for a child to attend, the priority system operated by the nursery for admissions, and the procedure by which a parent or parent in conjunction with a worker applies for a child to be admitted.

Given the range of information required by social workers, particularly intake workers, the problem then becomes how such information is made available, and what systems can be devised to do this more effectively. Streatfield and Mullings (1979), in a research programme designed to investigate the information needs of social services departments, comment on the fact that social services departments scarcely seem to exist as an entity, at least in the sense of organizations made up of people constantly communicating with one another. Social services staff interviewed found it difficult to conceptualize or relate to the department as a whole and limited their allegiance to their own particular workplace or team. Stevenson (1977) similarly found, in research into eight local authority and two hospital social services departments, that many staff commented on the difficulties of communication in the large bureaucratic structures such departments have become, finding themselves to be highly dependent on face-to-face contact for effective communication. They adhered to the ideal that 'small is beautiful', and some teams increased their own cohesion by their opposition to 'the enemy at the door'; as often as not the headquarters of the social services department as the traditional enemies of Housing and the Department of Health and Social Security.

Communication, therefore, takes place primarily orally, either face-to-face or by telephone. Meetings are also viewed as an important means of obtaining information. Streatfield and Mullings (1979) found that social workers exchange advice, information, and opinions freely among peers in their own team, but there was little communication between different area teams at fieldworker level, with the disadvantage that experiences were not shared. For example, one area team may develop a new strategy in dealing with fuel debts which could usefully be taken up by other area teams, but such information is not usually made freely available as a result of the relative insularity of work teams.

Staff at higher hierarchical levels are more likely to be in frequent communication through meetings and working parties, but at such events are more likely to be concerned with matters of planning and policy than day-to-day functioning and basic fieldwork problems. Researchers found that they observed little systematic information seeking although the giving, receiving, seeking, and exchanging of information went on all the time to the extent that Streatfield and Mullings commented that a cynic might argue that social services departments existed primarily to handle information. The view that social services staff preferred informal methods of communication was substantiated with the finding that 60 per cent of 'information events' were either conversations or telephone calls.

The results of research undertaken substantiate the belief that, at least at field level, information collecting is a fairly haphazard venture dependent on oral communication. Much valuable time was wasted in checking with others about whether a correct procedure had been laid down and if so what it consisted of, and also of who is eligible for what service or benefit. Similar difficulties were found in relation to basic information about local organizations and key community figures, with social workers checking with other team members to ascertain the relevant facts about whether certain organizations exist, the name, address, and telephone number of the person to contact, and other such details.

Neill (1976) found in 1975 that 75 per cent of social workers interviewed felt they needed to know more about the resources in their own community, and 50 per cent also wanted more information about legal matters and treatment skills. There was felt to be a general lack of ready information about resources. Similarly, Streatfield (1979) found that 66 per cent of staff interviewed said they found it difficult to obtain the necessary information to do their jobs, especially procedural information, legal information, and news of developments in social work. This problem is increased when considering the needs of the whole department, since information needs vary dramatically with different work roles. Even when comparing the needs of intake and long-term teams the former require a much greater amount and range of hard factual data about community resources, whereas the latter are likely to need detailed information on children's and hostel placements, given that long-term case loads tend to consist primarily of statutory work with children in care.

The problem of finding the required information is particularly acute for social workers who are unsure as to who does what and how to do it, and have to learn to establish and make use of the informal network of contacts that are so important to effective functioning. Most social workers were found to claim to have specialized knowledge about some aspect of work and to regularly share this information with other team members. A tremendous amount of information is, therefore, present in social services departments, the problem being where it is located and how it can be organized systematically so as to be generally available. The tendency is for different individuals to hold particular pieces of information which are elicited only if the worker needing the information happens to communicate with the person who holds it.

Streatfield found that official stores of information of all kinds, whether in procedure manuals, libraries, or filing systems, were rudimentary in nature and generally little used by staff. 33 per cent of staff kept their own stores of information, being dissatisfied with that held by the department. Since social services departments rely heavily on the correct application of procedures, and a substantial amount of time is spent at field level in ascertaining who to contact and how, for example, to go about receiving a child into care or admitting an elderly person to a residential home, one of the solutions has been seen to be the compiling of procedure manuals. Such manuals should be designed as a guide to social workers about such basic but time-consuming tasks as what forms to fill in for what services and where to send them. They may also contain the relevant criteria for eligibility for a service and what legislation the service falls under. They are not intended as, and should not include, a guide to practice. Many procedure manuals do, however, fall into the trap of trying to be both a guide to good social work practice as well as a guide to departmental procedures. As such they become confusing, cumbersome, and unwieldy and lose credibility with the staff they are designed to help. Matters of social work practice are the province of the supervisor, not the matter for a step-by-step guide. Streatfield and Mullings's research has confirmed the impression that procedure manuals have not been an unqualified success as an answer to the problem of providing a clear and readily available source of information about departmental procedures. Two reasons are advanced for this.

Firstly, those given the responsibility for compiling and – equally important – updating the manual rate such a task as low-priority, boring, and time-consuming work. Secondly, the manuals are often composed by those who lack either the imagination or the experience to put themselves in a position of one trying to read and apply the procedures. Even where relatively competent and comprehensive manuals have been compiled, unless they are regularly reviewed and updated they soon become out of date and once again lose credibility with social work staff. To overcome the battle to persuade staff to use such manuals, which if properly produced would be a welcome asset, they need to be both relevant and trustworthy. The production of adequate procedure manuals and local directories of resources, statutory and voluntary, would do much to decrease the amount of time spent seeking basic information and to reduce the flow of inconsistent and contradictory information.

Streatfield and Mullings (1979) conclude their work with a series of suggestions with the object of improving the availability of information in social services departments. Firstly, they suggest that the uncontrolled flow of paper through departments should be curtailed. The effect of endless bulletins, circulars, minutes of meetings, and the like is to swamp the individual with so much information as to render him incapable of retaining it or relating it to other relevant material; as an alternative, better-equipped departmental libraries would be able to provide specific services to key groups of staff who could then act as gatekeeper by passing the information to the relevant colleagues. This would be a way of meeting the different needs of staff in different roles within the department.

Specialist advisers, as employed in many departments, could play a more active role in the dissemination of information about their area of work. Such specialist staff – the product of an attempt to maintain areas of expertise dissipated when social work 'went generic' after the Seebohm reorganization – are often in a somewhat ambiguous position. Generally being located centrally they are not an integral part of area teams, but likewise have an unclear position in line management. Their role is, therefore, often unclear and social workers are left unsure as to how to use their services. They are, however, in a prime position to provide information dissemination and training in their specialism. A departmental consultancy list that would identify official and unofficial experts in various fields would also be a useful addition to information activities, which play such an important part.

The co-ordination of the production of information leaflets and the development of standard information packs – for example on adoption, fostering, and non-accidental injury – would reduce the duplication of effort sometimes caused by such endeavours and provide staff with readily available, subject-related information. A re-examination of the role of departmental newsletter may offer a possibility for the dissemination of information, as does the development of in-service training sessions devoted to specific areas of work or legislation – for example, the Children's Act 1975.

All these suggestions, and others, highlight the importance of efficient and effective information-handling systems in social services departments. With the reorganization and growth of social services departments the case emerges for such departments to employ specialist information officers. Information officers employed at a suitable level within social services departments could play a key role in developing adequate and effective ways of conveying the basic operational information required by field staff, and in the production of such things as procedure manuals and local directories. Their role would also bring them into close contact with the training element in the department. More-effective communication, although not necessarily in greater quantity, is vital to providing better client services, and information provision cannot be divorced from the whole area of work in social services. As Streatfield concludes: 'We believe that by paying more attention to the provision of adequate information services at all levels, social services departments will be better equipped to serve their clients' (Streatfield 1979: 12).

The relationship of intake teams to other local resources

One of the objectives of the Seebohm reorganization was that the new social services departments should not stand in isolation from the surrounding community, but rather should constitute one element in a network of services available to the community. Such a network would consist of statutory and voluntary agencies, as well as local community organizations and the increasing number of self-help groups. As intake workers stand as gatekeepers for both their own department and other agencies, it is crucial that such workers have both an adequate knowledge of community resources and the ability to build up relationships with these other agencies. It is not only a question of knowing what agencies and groups exist but also something about what they deal with, and how they work. For example, to know that there is a locally based Family Service Unit does not help the worker when considering referring a family to that unit. Additional information is necessary, such as what type of cases the unit deal with and how they organize their work. If they work particularly with young children, including running childrens' groups and playschemes, there is probably little point in referring a family with grown-up children living at home.

Similarly, when considering referring perhaps an elderly person to a housing association due to open some units of sheltered accommodation in the area, it is advisable to know some details about how the scheme is to be run and what the criteria are for consideration. If the association is prepared to accept only those under 70 years of age, there is little point in referring a client who is older.

An inadequate knowledge of the functioning of other agencies leads to mis-referrals and causes the client yet further anxiety and frustration. All too often intake workers are at the end of just such chains of mis-referrals, and faced with understandably angry and upset clients who feel they have been passed from pillar to post through a series of other agencies. Take for example the client who is receiving supplementary benefit and is in need of clothing. They may first of all approach the information section at the town hall, who advise them to go along to the Department of Health and Social Security. Social security, however, are very busy and short-staffed and as the client is now becoming a little upset at being kept waiting suggest that the client approaches the social services. The client, there-fore, arrives at the area office, all too often the wrong one and probably after two to three hours' effort, and asks to see someone about some clothes. The intake worker's initial reaction, understandably, is to send the client straight back to social security. However, given that the client has now been to three agencies, to send them off again without an explanation as to where they should go, what to ask for, and how to go about it will probably lead to either a further pointless visit or else the client giving up altogether.

The intake worker is, therefore, likely to advise the client and possibly undertake advocating on his or her behalf. This common situation highlights the need for intake workers to have a firm grasp of the role and work of other agencies in the community and be able to advise the client accordingly. All too often intake social workers undertake work with a client simply because other agencies are not fulfilling their functions. Being so often at the receiving end of a chain of mis-referrals, and experiencing the frustration and anger this causes both worker and client, serves to emphasize the im-portance of building up an adequate knowledge of the role and function of other agencies, and consequently both gives the client a better service and reduces the frustration caused by having to deal with inappropriate referrals.

Decisions taken about new referrals by intake workers are not made in a vacuum, nor solely on the basis of an assessment of the needs of the client. Decisions made by social workers in social services departments are coloured by the availability of the relevant resources. This is equally true of intake and long-term workers, but particularly marked in the case of intake workers by virtue of the volume of requests for services of all kinds dealt with. The know-ledge of resources necessary to function effectively consists not only of the concrete services – such as the availability of home-help time, day-care places for the elderly, residential accommodation, day-nursery places, foster-parents and children's-home vacancies – but also the availability of social work time.

Clients are not allocated to social workers only on the basis of an assessment of their problems and a decision about the potential for change; the other major element in allocation is the work load the team is carrying, and whether there is a social worker available and able to accept the case. Statutory child-care work invariably takes the highest priority for allocation and consequently in times of staff shortages and overall lack of adequate staffing levels, work with a high preventive potential but on matters not presenting particular problems at referral tends to be left. Such factors as this have considerable influence on the behaviour of intake workers; when the long-term social workers in the area team are unable to take on any more work, intake workers are likely to react by dealing with clients more and more on a 'one-off' or short-term basis, since there are no other avenues open to them within the team. There is consequently an increased tendency to take a narrow approach and deal only with the presenting problem, because to do more is likely to unleash needs and expectations that cannot then be met.

If, however, a new social work post has just been established, or there is a team member returning from a course, or a student is about to arrive on placement, the intake worker is likely to perceive this as an element of slack in the system and be more likely to assess cases with a view to their receiving social work help. This knowledge and perception of the availability of resources of all kinds, therefore, plays a major part in the assessment activities of intake workers. When there is a marked shortage of residential care for the elderly in comparison with the level of need, requests for residential care are likely to be handled in a quite different way to when resources are adequate.

The lack of resources of all kinds generally experienced by social services departments makes it necessary to develop a clear and explicit set of priorities as to what work can and cannot be undertaken. The idea of allocating resources according to explicit criteria requires that rational and systematic assessment of need be maintained and emphasizes the importance of intake workers developing their assessment skills. Staff need to have a clear view of the department's priorities and resource availability and to be able to confidently translate these into practice. As well as this, intake workers require a high degree of knowledge not only of their own department's capability but also of local and national resources. This is particularly likely to play a part in those cases where the department is unable to offer help either because the request is considered low priority or because of lack of resources. Knowledge of such alternative resources ranges from voluntary social work agencies for social work help and charities for financial assistance to housing associations for accommodation difficulties and self-help groups for particular personal problems.

Intake workers, therefore, require a wide range of knowledge about other resources which may be able to help clients. Indeed, in some cases it may be more appropriate that the client seeks help elsewhere. The intake worker's job, therefore, includes a high degree of consultation and collaboration with other professionals, officials, and volunteers. As well as establishing what help the client needs, what role it is appropriate for the worker to play, and what other agency or group may be more appropriate to help, as Rees points out: 'In addition, social workers at all levels of management must be clear about which clients' situations are part of a larger social problem with local and national political implications and should not, therefore, be treated merely as a single case' (Rees 1974: 277).

The development of the unitary model as a theory of social work practice, formalizing at a conceptual level what had previously been an unformulated element of practice, has served to further emphasize the need for the worker to be aware of the broader ramifications of particular problems. The worker needs to assess problems on a broad canvas and often then to act as an active go-between in mediation between client groups and social institutions. Although the individual worker need not be competent to intervene in all the social systems affecting a particular problem, he does require the ability to judge what kind of expertise is needed and who should be included and consequently to have the capacity to work in collaboration with practitioners of various orientations, consultants, administrators, and para-professionals. Specialist practitioners tend to define problems in terms of their own specialism; for example, a caseworker is likely to define problems as arising within the individual whereas a community worker is more likely to perceive problems as being rooted in social institutions.

The intake worker especially, therefore, needs to be able to assess problems broadly and plan intervention flexibly. This is seen by Vickery (1977) as a trend towards generalism, carrying with it the danger of encouraging the training of a professional who knows a little about a lot of things, but lacks particular specialist skills. She further fears that an emphasis on the unitary approach in assessing problems may obscure the need for adequate knowledge in specific fields. If basic professional training is designed to teach a generalist approach in fields of practice then she stresses the need for specialist knowledge and methods of work to be developed after qualification. Whilst there is clearly a need for specialist workers to develop expertise in particular areas and methods of work, this tendency to denigrate the generalist worker devalues the extensive range of knowledge, skills, and expertise required – particularly by intake workers – to facilitate adequate assessments which enable the worker to offer the client the most appropriate form of help. Because the generalist worker has to communicate in rapid succession with a wide variety of different agencies and organizations, he needs access to information built up over a considerable period of contact and such information has, therefore, to be built up on a team basis and shared. In addition to knowledge of formal organizations, there is also a range of knowledge of informal local networks and community groups which can prove invaluable in the course of day-to-day work.

While there thus seems to be a permanent and lasting role for generalist intake workers in local authority social services departments, if they are to continue to spend a substantial proportion of their time in assessing new referrals and then making decisions about the appropriate form of social work intervention the question arises as to how such intervention is to be organized. It would appear that the tide is now turning away from the generic boom which theoretically followed Seebohm reorganization, and more and more departments are looking into the employment of specialist staff in some areas. As Younghusband (1978a) has pointed out, by the mid-1970s, cuts in public spending and nil-growth policies were affecting social services departments who still emanated an air of general confusion as to their aims, boundaries, priorities, and ability to give a professional service. At the same time voluntary organizations had made great strides. An increasing amount of voluntary effort existed both locally and nationally to provide general co-ordination of specific services for particular groups of people, one of their functions being to provide specialist services as a part of the resources available to social workers. Commenting on the difficulties encountered by social workers in large, bureaucratic social services departments, Stevenson says:

'My great fear is of a situation in which the great majority of social workers are employed in a setting which gives them increasingly less satisfaction, so that the vocational rewards are sought else-where, perhaps in the voluntary sector, where specialized in-itiatives are increasingly encouraged.'

(Stevenson 1977: 14)

This apparent tendency for movement from generalist local authority social services departments into more specialist employ-ment in the voluntary field can also be explained by the fact that fieldwork expertise and experience has not hitherto been recognised by local authority departments as a means of career advancement, the latter having been primarily related to stepping onto the management ladder. Specialist workers have, therefore, lost out to managers in the local-authority field.

Intake workers are dependent on a network of other resources both within the department and in the community, in order to offer clients an effective service. Because of the range of problems dealt with by intake teams, a relatively high proportion of cases are not requiring specific specialist social work help but fall more into the area of wanting information, advice, and counselling. If it becomes the case that those clients who do require specialist social work help cannot be accommodated within the work load of the social services depart-ment, whether due to lack of expertise in the department, pressure of statutory work, or shortage of staff, then the effects on professional social work are likely to be wide reaching. As Bamford has stated:

'Is it inconceivable that British welfare provision will follow the American model with low-quality, low-status public welfare services dealing predominantly with financial difficulties while voluntary agencies undertake the innovative, specialist and pro-fessionally satisfying social work?'

(Bamford 1977: 1)

6

The relationship of social work theory to intake work

Introduction

Intake teams were originally established as a pragmatic, organizational response to the problems facing area teams after reorganization. Indeed, their prime *raison d'être* was to protect the quality of long-term social work practice, which was suffering as a result of the high level of bombardment area teams experienced, resulting in social workers rushing from one crisis to the next and having little time left to plan and innovate in their work with long-term cases. Casework, based on the psychodynamic models imported from the USA, was still the order of the day and the model of social work practice which laid claim to high status.

Intake teams, with their remit to deal with new and short-term work and with an investment in dealing with client problems speedily in a business-like, competent manner, were not hailed as an innovatory professional social work response. Accordingly, they initially tended to be viewed as rather low status, and in some areas intake work was likened to a clerical function. Intake teams were slow to pick up and use the developments in professional social work theory that would validate their aims and objectives, justify the model in which they were working, and further benefit clients. Well before 1970, in the USA, there were developments that carried considerable potential as practice methods that could be taken up by intake teams. Crisis intervention, various models of short-term work, and the development of the unitary model all have a broad range of application to British social work practice, but all bear particular relevance to practice in those teams established and developed for the purpose of providing a short-term and crisis service to clients. Intake teams need, therefore, to explicitly incorporate such methods of work to give sound professional standing to their organizational advantages. As long as this is not the case, there remains the possibility that intake teams will be viewed as no more than an interim organizational response to reorganization, rather than a professional social work service in its own right.

Traditional distinctions in local authority social work practice

Social work practice in Britain has traditionally been defined primarily in terms of the client group served. Before the Seebohm reorganization distinctions were relatively clearly defined; social workers were either child care officers, welfare officers, mental welfare officers, medical social workers, or psychiatric social workers. In addition, they were either caseworkers, groupworkers, or community workers. The individual workers' professional identity was, therefore, generally derived from the combination of client group and method of practice. Social work practice is profoundly influenced by the organizational setting within which it is located, and divisions or specializations tend to arise out of the necessity of having to divide the knowledge, skills, and tasks required of the worker into manageable units. Specialization in local authority social work before the Seebohm reorganization was based on client group served, although even within the defined boundaries of the Children's, Welfare, and Mental Welfare Departments there was the possibility of individual workers specializing further. For example, child care officers may specialize in adoption work, mental welfare officers in the rehabilitation of long-stay patients, or welfare officers in problems of homelessness.

Despite the different locations in which social workers were situated, the prime method of practice used was casework. Casework theory is largely derived from psycho-analytic principles, particularly Freudian theory and the subsequent development of ego psychology. There have been three major schools of thought in casework theory: the diagnostic school, as propounded by Hollis; the problem-solving school of Perlman; and the functional school of which Smalley is an advocate. Although there exist basic differences between these schools, all three are firmly rooted within a dynamic psychological frame of reference. All these theoretical schools of casework were initially developed in the USA, where the system for the provision of a social work service is radically different from that in Britain, most social work agencies being in the voluntary sector and offering a private service to fee-paying clients. Contrastingly, in Britain – where nearly all social workers are employed by local authorities – the social control and caretaker functions of social workers are much more apparent and it is logical to assume that the motivation of many clients may not be as high as where they are voluntarily electing to apply for a service they are charged for. Despite this fundamental difference in the organization of social work services, casework was adopted in Britain as the basic method used by social workers.

Owing to its origins in psycho-analytic theory and ego psychology, casework – hence much of social work – has developed with an innately individualist bias, often viewing problems as the result of individual failings or pathology and, therefore, requiring 'treatment'. Such a treatment approach, as exemplified by Hollis and the diagnostic school, works from a notion whereby the worker is responsible for assessing, diagnosing, and then treating the pathological condition of the client. Such a model of treatment relied upon practice that was generally of a long-term and psychodynamic nature, the object often seeming to be to effect a 'cure'.

Social work practice in Britain can thus be seen to have been greatly influenced by theoretical schools developed in the USA, casework being viewed as high-status work carried out by qualified social workers in their own particular setting. Between the different professional social work bodies there sometimes seemed to be an implicit ranking, with psychiatric social workers accruing higher status than other workers, perhaps as a result of the greater degree of casework skill felt to be required in their practice. Although well before the 1970s generic social work courses were being developed, many training courses continued to take note of, and hence direct some of their teaching towards, the different departments to which students would be returning, and this, therefore, contributed to the degree of specialization that existed in social work before the Seebohm reorganization.

With the Seebohm Report this changed. Generic departments broke down the distinctions between the old specialist areas of work, although many workers continued, and continue today, to carry case loads with a bias towards a particular client group. In addition to the breakdown of the divisions between the departments, the new social services departments were confronted with unforeseen demands which had been unleashed as a result of reorganization (see Chapter 1). The initial result was that workers placed under tremendous pressure from the demands made upon them were unable to continue with established long-term models of practice and had to concentrate more on short-term and crisis intervention. This was often viewed as a negative consequence of the new generic departments, such intervention being seen as palliative in nature, rather than as an opportunity to innovate and use new models of intervention. Out of the disenchantment with the fate of long-term work, intake teams were developed, offering a primarily problem-focused service, often dealing exclusively with the presenting problem, undertaking much more information and advice work, covering a very broad range of problems and, in most teams, providing a short-term social work service.

The setting up of social services departments at the beginning of the 1970s came soon after the extensive controversies of the previous decade in the social work profession on the development and relative merits of different methods of work, what Younghusband sees as:

'the slow development of conceptualized groupwork compared with casework, followed by the boisterous arrival of community work in the late 1960s. . . . The joint effect of this and of widened responsibilities in social services and social work departments (and indeed in the penal system) was that social work lost grip of its identity . . . by the mid-1970s it had not found a clear professional identity between the poles of social action and psychotherapy.'

(Younghusband 1978a: 28)

The traditional underpinning of social work practice in Britain had been removed. Not only were there no longer the clear distinctions in agency function, but there was confusion about the methods used. Casework, groupwork, and community work were vying with each other for professional acclaim, and even traditional casework practice was coming under attack from the new demands facing social workers in area teams, such that the established long-term methods of work were being set aside out of necessity in favour of short-term and crisis approaches. The development of area teams incorporating intake and long-term teams has caused the major functional distinction in such teams to be between intake and long-term social work practice. Given the preponderance of statutory and voluntary surveillance, monitoring, and caretaking activities undertaken by social services departments, primarily by long-term teams owing to the nature of the work, the sort of work undertaken and hence the social work methods used could be expected to differ greatly from that in intake teams.

Intake workers are located at a point in the area team structure where they are required to deal with a wide diversity of needs and demands incorporating all client groups. There is comparatively little likelihood of an intake worker specializing in a particular client group in terms of having a preponderance of that client group on his case load. This is not to say that intake workers may not develop a particular interest in and expertise with a particular client group or category of problem, but this is likely to be only one aspect of a much more generic field of practice. The Service Delivery Study (DHSS 1975), examining social work practice in 1973 (soon after re-organization), found the most worrying aspect at that time to be that social workers trained for long-term skilled work were being forced to concentrate on short-term and crisis work as a result of the very high referral rate and variety of requests made to the departments. Social work specialization, however, was described as diluted but not abandoned.

Similarly, Stevenson (1978), reporting on a research project into the organization and practice of social service teams seven years after reorganization, found that despite the amalgamation of the different departments, many social workers do still specialize informally to a greater or lesser extent in work with particular client groups, reflecting the past agency divisions. The same study revealed relatively little specialization by method of work. The overall category under which most social work practice fell was that of casework, broadly defined. More specifically, in a study undertaken under the auspices of the Department of Health and Social Security into the practitioner's view of social service teams, it was said of social work activities: 'The casework approach, then, was one which not only recognised multiple causation of problems but, in turn, drew from a number of specific techniques of intervention and cast the social worker in a number of different roles' (DHSS 1978: 115). Social workers were found not to concentrate solely on either casework aimed at forming therapeutic relationships to explore feelings and change attitudes to the exclusion of practical difficulties, nor to be reliant wholly on the 'service provision' end of the spectrum. 'Instead, they seemed to be eclectic in their methods and focused on the psychological, social and material causes of problems' (DHSS 1978: 116). Specialization, therefore, to the extent that it exists in local authority social work, appears to focus on client group rather than method of work. However, whilst this may be the case in relation to long-term teams the emergence of intake teams with a remit to undertake all new and short-term work suggests that in such teams at least the social work methods used may provide the specialist input, rather than the client group served, for all client groups present at intake and it is how the problems they present are dealt with which provides the essence of intake work. There still exists considerable tension and confusion in workers' minds about the comparative advantages and disadvantages of long-term and short-term work. The Department of Health and Social Security study found:

'Quite different opinions were expressed about these two types of work; some associated short-term work with higher status and more "movement" whilst long-term work was seen as "less high powered" and not achieving much change. Others viewed short-term work as "second best" and equated long-term work with "in-depth" work.'

(DHSS 1978: 154)

The reorganization of local authority social services departments and the establishment of generic area teams, with the subsequent development in many areas of a model comprising intake and long-term teams, virtually paralleled and mutually interacted with developments in the field of casework theory and practice. The approaches used at the end of the 1970s and early 1980s are dramatically different from those used ten years earlier. Three broad areas have had an especially large effect over the past decade, and all have particular relevance to the practice of social work in intake teams: crisis intervention; short-term, task-centred, and contract work; and the development of the unitary model.

These models of practice appear to have developed quite independently of the development of intake teams as a means of organizing to provide an efficient and effective service. However, the development of such models of practice – which are all essentially short term, time limited, and problem focused – can be seen to lend professional backing to what was originally a pragmatic, organizational measure taken because of the heavy bombardment experienced by area-team social workers after reorganization, and the consequent fate of long-term work. While these models of practice are particularly relevant to intake work, where they should ideally form the basis of practice, they are also of use to workers in long-term teams, where they can provide a framework and focus for work within a long-term case and hence assist in avoiding the tendency for unplanned, vague 'supportive' long-term work with no clear goals and hence no means of assessing whether social work intervention is achieving anything with a particular family or situation. The use of such models in intake work can be argued as raising intake from an organizational and pragmatic response to a professional response in terms of social work theory and models of practice.

The use of crisis intervention

Intake teams, established to deal with new incoming work, are at the point within their agency where it is most likely that they will undertake crisis work with individuals and families. 'Crisis', however, is a word in common parlance in the English language, and it is questionable to what extent workers use the phrase crisis intervention in a loosely descriptive way rather than in describing a specific method of social work practice with its own theoretical framework and principles of practice. Crisis intervention was originally developed within the field of preventive psychiatry, and it is mental-health work that has continued to be primarily influenced by it. Caplan views preventive psychiatry as part of a much wider community endeavour:

> 'My emphasis on a comprehensive approach is based on the belief that not only are mentally disordered behaviour patterns part of a whole system of ecological responses of a population in its interaction with its environment, but that our own operations as preventive psychiatrists are also a part of the total community security system whereby socially deviant responses and undue individual victimization are kept in check. To ensure professional effectiveness, we must . . . take care not to erect boundaries which artificially fragment the field itself.'
>
> (Caplan 1964: 18)

He goes on to divide prevention into the now familiar primary, secondary, and tertiary areas.

Primary prevention aims at reducing the incidence of mental disorder in the community and thus focuses on group and community processes and support systems rather than on the individual. It is consequently directed towards non-specific helping resources and conditions believed to be harmful. Such conditions include biological and role transitions which produce major crises among a significant percentage of the population – for example birth, puberty, marriage, illness, and death – particularly in cultural settings where there is no ritualized means of dealing with such events with group support. Preventive psychiatry, therefore, finds a focus for practice in particular locations to which individuals and families in crisis will probably turn, such as obstetric, accident, and surgical units of hospitals. Kaplan and Mason (1965), for example, discuss the particular problems facing mothers with premature babies and identify this as an important location for preventive work. Similarly, Bellak and Small (1965) advocate pre- and post-operative psychotherapy where certain operations arouse specific and largely predictable problems, as in cases of amputation or hysterectomy.

Such primary preventive intervention and anticipatory guidance can be seen to be desirable and in the long-term economical in reducing the numbers of individuals who develop long-term disorders as a result of their relative isolation at the time of crisis, when both the motivation of the individual and the influence of the worker are likely to be highly conducive to a successful outcome.

Secondary prevention aims at reducing the duration of mental illness by earlier diagnosis and effective treatment, and depends upon a sharpening of diagnostic tools, a revision of agency-intake procedure, and public information about the services available. Caplan emphasizes 'Those treatment methods that demand least psychiatric time and that involve a maximum of indirect therapy mediated by community care-givers backed up by mental health consultants' (Caplan 1964: 108) to prevent hospitalization, wherever possible.

Tertiary prevention, aimed at reducing the effects of residual defects for those suffering from psychiatric disorders and increasing their social effectiveness, depends on a carefully planned and comprehensive development of community facilities to make community care a reality.

Although originally formulated for mental-health work and preventive psychiatry, crisis theory and its application in practice has much to offer social work. Intake workers are less likely at present to be working in the area of primary prevention, although may well deal with cases referred soon after the crisis, for example distressed mothers returning home after the premature birth of their child, patients discharged from hospital after major surgery, or with bereaved individuals and families. While the ideal of developing community-based facilities to help individuals confronted by such life crises is laudable, in many cases it is at present more likely that the individual or family will be referred or find their way to social services given the lack of such community support. Secondary prevention is the area where intake workers are highly likely to figure, not solely in mental-health cases but in many and varied situations where an individual or family are experiencing some sort of crisis and where rapid and effective intervention times – such that the client's motivation and the worker's influence are at a maximum – may serve to reduce the long-term deleterious effects of the crisis. Tertiary prevention again is an area where community resources are at a premium, and while social workers have a part to play they are largely dependent on the resources available to them to plan a realistic programme of community care for a variety of client groups: the elderly, the handicapped, and children, as well as the mentally ill.

Perlman's problem-solving model of social casework (1970) stands firmly upon the belief that life is a problem-encountering, problem-solving process, and sees the problem-solving model of casework as designed to help individuals and families cope with or resolve some difficulty they are currently finding insurmountable, in ways that will maximize their conscious effort and competence. The by-product of such practice is that the individual or family is then hopefully better able to cope with future problems. As such, there seems to be a close theoretical and practical affinity between such a model and that of crisis intervention. Both can be said to be firmly grounded in psycho-analytic personality theory, and crisis intervention particularly uses such theory in combination with selected social science concepts and hence is increasingly aware of the individual or family in their social environment and uses this as the unit of attention in psychosocial treatment. In addition to the greater emphasis placed on the social milieu in crisis intervention, this model also takes up and develops the theme of short-term intervention. When crisis theory was being formulated in the 1950s and 1960s, long-term treatment was very much the style of choice. Austin, in her foreword to Parad's reader on crisis intervention, comments:

'Short-term treatment has been discussed chiefly as a matter of expediency; seldom has it been recommended as a treatment of choice. One can foresee that this attitude towards brief therapy may change under the impact of the crisis formulations, which include new assumptions about the meaning of the "precipitating event" and its significance for focusing the problems to be treated. These formulations describe the dynamics for change that are mobilized under stress and that are more accessible to intervention at the point the client comes for help than they are likely to be at a later point.'

(Austin 1965: xi)

Crisis intervention as a mode of practice arises, therefore, out of the fusion of concepts of crisis and concepts of brief treatment.

Rapoport says of crisis intervention:

'It exists as a framework for viewing individuals and families in situations of urgency and stress, and as an approach it leads to the generation of useful practice principles applicable to both clinical work and modes of primary prevention in mental health work.'

(Rapoport 1970: 267)

Crisis can be defined as an upset in a steady state and crisis theory is based on the postulate that individuals strive to maintain a state of equilibrium with a constant series of adaptive manoeuvres and characteristic problem-solving activities.

Three interrelated factors combine to produce a state of crisis: there exist one or a series of hazardous events which pose some threat; there is a threat to current or past instinctual needs, which may be symbolically linked to earlier threats, that result in vulnerability or conflict; and there is an inability to respond with adequate coping mechanisms, characteristic problem-solving activities being insufficient to the hazard or threat. Intake workers are often presented with what can thus properly be defined as crises, and consequently are in a position to use crisis-intervention techniques as their chosen approach.

Comparatively common examples of crises presented at intake include the family where the adolescent daughter becomes pregnant and the family are then unable to cope with the threat this poses to their hitherto united state; the discharge from hospital of a family member who has just suffered a paralysing illness, necessitating the re-negotiation of roles within the family; or the reception into care of children whose mother, for example, is admitted to hospital for either a physical or psychiatric illness – the separation from the parent causing a crisis for the children, who need the opportunity to work through their feelings. Such an opportunity may be provided by friends, relatives, or foster-parents; but where this is not the case, for whatever reason, the children need help to prevent their developing pathological defences.

The central feature of crises are that they are time limited, usually lasting no longer than four to six weeks. Individuals and families cannot sustain themselves in a state of crisis, and, therefore, work towards re-establishing some level of stability and equilibrium. Crises, therefore, blow over; what is crucial is the comparison of the level of functioning before and after the crises. A crisis generally has four elements in its configuration. Firstly there is the precipitating event, often known as the stress or stressor. This event is then perceived as hazardous to the individual's or family's basic needs and goals, such as the need for security, affection, or bodily integrity. The response to this perceived hazardous event then results in the crisis. Finally comes the phase of resolution, when the individual or family, or indeed the group or community, is helped towards adaptive and away from maladaptive solutions. Intervention, therefore, has the dual objectives of reducing the impact of the stressful events, and using the crisis to help those affected learn new and more effective ways of coping with the present as well as subsequent crises. Crises can, therefore, be said to evoke images not only of danger but also of opportunity.

The hallmark of crisis intervention is the preventive potential which it embodies coupled with the increased potential for change of individuals or families in a crisis state. Again, much of the work undertaken has been in relation to the field of mental illness and the prevention of hospital admissions. Numerous psychiatric hospitals and mental health programmes in America and to a lesser extent in this country are including crisis-intervention services, generally multi-disciplinary teams of workers who work in the community to prevent hospitalization. Parad observes that the increased emphasis on community care with its concomitant practice of the discharge of long-stay patients is likely to increase the need for locally based emergency mental health programmes, as moderate pressure on an ex-patient, such as perhaps caused by the strains felt by family and community resources, may cause a crisis and the danger of re-admission.

Langsley *et al.* (1971) undertook a study on the effectiveness of family crisis intervention in preventing admission to a psychiatric hospital. Three hundred patients, diagnosed by psychiatrists as needing immediate hospitalization, were randomly assigned to two groups. Group 1 were treated with a family crisis intervention approach while group 2 were immediately hospitalized. Results of follow-up studies showed that those in group 1 were significantly less likely to be rehospitalized than those in group 2. Follow-ups at six and eighteen months showed no difference in social adaptations or ability to cope with life's crises between the two groups. Those in group 1, when they did need admission to hospital, were found to be hospitalized for a significantly shorter period. It would seem, therefore, that the family crisis intervention approach had shown its preventive potential by reducing the number of subsequent crises experienced by the families so treated.

There are three central questions which the worker must consider when embarking on crisis work: what is troubling the client or family; why do they come for help now; and what can I do to help? These three aspects are also central to intake work to clarify the problems being presented. Rapoport expands on this in terms of the worker's assessment:

'A major, initial diagnostic task is to develop quickly some working hypotheses about the nature of the crisis, the relevant precipitating stress or stresses, the general adaptive capacity of the individual and reasons for present impairment or inability to cope, as well as the extent and degree of his dysfunction. The next step is to appraise his potentialities for adaptive responses and the availability of salient internal, intrafamiliar, and community resources that can be mobilized quickly in order to restore some sense of equilibrium.'

(Rapoport 1970: 280)

The goals of intervention based on this assessment are the relief of the client's symptoms, the restoration of the client to the optimum level of functioning that existed before the present crisis (helping the client to understand the relevant precipitating events that contributed to the state of disequilibrium), and the identification of remedial measures that can be taken by the client or family or that are available through community resources. Given that crisis is a time-limited phenomenon, the timing of intervention is an important issue – the closer the intervention is to the time of the crisis, the greater the likelihood of a successful outcome. In addition to the crisis state itself being of a limited duration because of its very nature, crisis intervention is designed as a form of brief treatment. In common with other forms of brief treatment the worker's role is a much more active one, directed towards fostering the client's own mastery of his or her situation and avoiding regression, in contrast to the passive role generally taken by workers in long-term casework. Crisis workers are more likely to give advice, be directive, and use techniques involving confrontation interviews being highly focused rather than diffuse. Related to the more active role of the worker is the importance of his enthusiasm and optimism, which conveys a hope of resolution to the client.

When using brief treatment approaches the worker must genuinely accept that the goals of the work are limited, and that there is a clarity of expectations between client and worker, both needing to accept that the focal point throughout is the re-establishment in the client of a sense of autonomy.

Crisis intervention then, as a form of brief treatment based on the concept of crisis, is a model of practice which would appear highly relevant to intake workers in social services departments, despite the tendency for the model to be associated with mental-health work and preventive psychiatry. Many cases that are presented to intake teams can be viewed in terms of crisis theory, and hence should be amenable to time-limited crisis intervention techniques which would carry preventive potential.

It has been suggested that intake workers do not accept cases that are showing signs of, for example, early family breakdown – that is, those cases where social work intervention may achieve some resolution of difficulties before they become so entrenched as to become intractable. However, using the concept of crisis serves to focus attention on the precipitating events in a given situation and enable worker and client to concentrate on the resolution of the crisis in a way so as to maximize social functioning. In such a way, dealing with crises, which intake workers undeniably do, is extended into both a present resolution of difficulties and a prevention of responses which will prove maladaptive to the client's future functioning. The Department of Health and Social Security's project on social services teams (DHSS 1978), however, raised the question 'crisis for whom?' in relation to crisis work in area teams. Crises were loosely defined as situations demanding immediate action or intervention and hence often referred to a crisis for the worker or agency rather than the application of the concept of crisis to the client's problem. Consequently, social work intervention in cases was often directed towards allaying the worker's own anxiety and was, therefore, often aimed at the solution of immediate practical problems. Little effort seemed to be made by workers to differentiate between the urgency of the external circumstances and the emotional state of the client. The common responses to crises did not, therefore, comply with the basic tenets of the crisis-intervention model whereby the goal of

intervention is not solely the resolution of the immediate problem
but also to enable clients to develop their own ability in problem
solving and to restore to them as soon as possible a sense of
autonomy, thereby enabling them to continue and deal with present
and future crises.

Indeed, the intervention of a worker who proceeds to resolve
immediate practical problems serves to detract from, rather than
help restore, the individual's sense of autonomy. Crisis intervention
as a specific method of social work intervention was not found to be
often used by respondents in the project. This finding relates to the
tendency discussed earlier for intake workers to deal solely with the
presenting problem. They might, therefore, deal with a crisis by
busily taking some practical action, as suggested above, and ignoring
the wider preventive implications. Alternatively, it could be argued
that many of the principles of practice embodied in crisis intervention are used by intake workers but because they tend to be
eclectic in the methods used they did not distinguish this particular
model as the one being employed. Whichever is the case, and there
are probably elements of both in practice, the more stringent
application of the principles of crisis intervention – incorporating the
elements of short-term focused work with preventive potential –
apparently has much to offer intake workers as a mode of practice,
and suggests that social work training for intake workers might
concentrate more on this area of practice.

Because the disturbance in personal equilibrium created by crisis
is limited to a few weeks the time available for initial intervention is
limited and requires flexibility in intake and allocation procedures.
Stevenson (1978) suggests that there are now many opportunities for
experiment in the division of work in area teams and sees one of the
possibilities to be the setting up of sub-teams to deal with crisis work
of any sort. Such a proposition presumably reflects a disenchantment or disappointment with the way that intake teams are
handling such work, for it is to this team that it would naturally fall.
In part, the reason for the apparent lack of expertise in this model of
practice found in intake teams can be said to arise as a result of such
teams being initially conceptualized as organizational rather than
professional units. If intake teams are to continue and develop it is
crucial that they concentrate on developing expertise in professional
practice related to their field of operation.

The rise and development of short-term work

In the same way that casework theory is grounded largely in the field of psycho-analysis, and crisis intervention as a social work method derives from the principles and practice of preventive psychiatry, so short-term work has its origins in developments in the field of psychotherapy. The practice of psychotherapy has traditionally tended to be based on the model of depth analysis, aiming to effect 'cure' by the restructuring of basic identities, rather than towards goals of symptom shredding, the alleviation of distress, and fostering improved functioning. During the 1960s the model of depth analysis as a realistic mode of treatment for the increasing number of individuals who were experiencing some form of emotional distress became more and more questionable. The Report of The Joint Commission on Mental Illness and Health estimated that in the early 1960s seventeen million people in the USA were suffering from emotional problems that required treatment. Such a finding – coupled with the increasing public awareness of, and concern about, mental-health problems – resulted in greater demands being made on mental-health services of all kinds. At the same time it was being noted by various authors (Frank 1973, Malan 1963) that analysis was becoming an even longer process, with the worker in an increasingly passive role. Early, and more successful, techniques in analysis included an active role for the worker, dramatic work with the patient often culminating in the 'confession' of some traumatic experience. Malan observed that in the 1960s it was still the case that workers often achieved a few dramatic successes early in their careers, which were not subsequently repeated. It can, therefore, be suggested that the increasing length of analysis may be attributed not to the greater complexity of the patient's problems, but rather to the decrease in the worker's zeal, the disappearance of the novelty effect, and the reduction of the need to proselytize as different theoretical schools gained wider recognition.

Considering the constraints of time, personnel, and resources on depth analysis a more realistic approach seemed to be to develop methods of short-term psychotherapeutic intervention aimed primarily at relieving distress rather than at the restructuring of the personality. Emergency and other forms of brief psychotherapy were thus designed to meet the demand for psychotherapeutic help in crises to prevent individuals being crippled by emotional disorder, thereby enabling them to continue functioning even if far from optimally until, in some cases, more extensive professional help was available. Such treatment also carries preventive potential in situations where immediate treatment, although brief, may forestall progression towards more serious and possibly chronic maladaptations. In brief work the worker takes a much more active role in relation to the patient, is required to plan and make decisions rapidly, and quickly understand the patient's communications. Such intervention, although basically aimed at improving the individual's psychodynamic state sufficiently to enable him to continue functioning, may in the longer term have the secondary effect of increasing his personal autonomy, or of helping him arrive at a point from which autonomous or natural healing proceeds.

Bellak and Small (1965) found that among patients admitted to the medical-surgical emergency room of a general hospital with symptoms of appendicitis or a heart attack many were found to be suffering from anxiety and panic reactions which could be successfully treated on a brief psychotherapeutic basis. The significant criteria in selecting cases which could be treated with brief psychotherapy was found to be not the relative mildness of the symptoms, as was sometimes claimed to be the case, but the individual's motivation for change as a result of subjectively felt distress, and the enthusiasm of the worker, which serves to facilitate the role induction of the patient and to encourage the development of congruent expectations between patient and worker in the therapeutic process. Where motivation on the part of the patient is not strongly felt, as is often the case with those suffering from 'character disorders', longer term treatment is likely to be required. There was initially considerable resistance to the use of the brief psychotherapeutic approach, resulting from the traditional reverence for the analytic process. Malan's work, however, demonstrated that such intervention could achieve far-reaching improvement not only in symptoms but also in the neurotic behaviour patterns of patients with extensive and relatively long-standing neuroses.

Developments in the field of brief psychotherapy served to question the traditional reverence accorded to long-term, in-depth models of analysis and psychotherapy and to establish the validity of short-term models of practice. Just as the excessive demands for

psychotherapeutic treatment stimulated the interest in and development of forms of brief treatment, so with casework. While caseworkers continued to be in short supply their clientele continued to
grow, causing workers to search for faster and more economical
methods of treatment.

In 1964 the Community Service Society of New York undertook a
field experiment which was to have major repercussions in the
development of social work theory and practice. They set out to test
the relative effectiveness of contrasting patterns of casework treatment on problems in family relations. The particularly significant
phase of the experiment was the comparison of a brief service of
fixed duration and an open-ended service that could be, and often
was, of extended duration. The findings of this study formed the
basis of Reid and Shyne's work, *Brief and Extended Casework* (1969).
The central issue of this work was the comparison of these two
different kinds of structures for interpersonal treatment of complex
psychosocial problems. In one structure – 'planned short-term
service' – the casework intervention was limited in advance in
relation to input and duration. The second structure – 'continued
service' – was based on an expectation that intervention would be of
fairly lengthy duration, although neither the client nor the worker
specified any predetermined limits as regards input or duration. The
style of work found in 'planned short-term service' cases was similar
to that later developed more fully in task-centred work. Reid and
Shyne see the core of short-term work as follows:

> 'perhaps the essential feature of planned short-term service treat-
> ment strategy was the attempt of the caseworkers to restrict the
> focus of treatment, if possible, to a key aspect of the problem for
> which help was being sought. With time at a premium, it seemed
> sounder to work intensively on a limited area than to attempt to
> relate to all facets of the family's problems. It was assumed that
> the problems given primary attention would be representative of
> the larger problems of the family. If the key area to be dealt with
> could provide a fulcrum, treatment might then be able to serve as
> a lever to promote changes in the family's problems as a whole.'
> (Reid and Shyne 1979: 63)

The evidence at the conclusion of the fieldwork experiment
suggested that the 'planned short-term service' model was the more

effective pattern of intervention. The 'continued service' model included a greater investment of cost, time, and energy on the part of the client, worker, and agency, yet there was no indication that this additional investment was compensated by additional benefits. 'Continued service' was apparently carried well beyond the point of diminishing returns, and was unable to improve on the outcomes of those clients receiving the briefer model of treatment. Reid and Shyne conclude:

> 'Evidence from the present experiment and other studies has suggested that planned short-term treatment may be at least as efficacious as open-ended, continued treatment for certain types of problems and a certain type of clientele, namely marital and child-related problems occurring within intact families who voluntarily seek help.'
>
> (Reid and Shyne 1969: 194)

The clientele worked with in the study, therefore, are at variance with a large proportion of the clientele of a local-authority social services team, where a substantial proportion of the work with families is of a statutory nature and requires the caretaking and social control functions of social workers. However, this does not detract from the established efficacy of planned short-term work. On the contrary, it serves to highlight the potential for meaningful, short-term intervention with a relatively high rate of success. Such a finding can be viewed as an incentive to social workers, particularly intake workers, to undertake some such work to experience the positive outcome so often lost to workers because of the chronic and intractable problems with which they are often faced. It can be argued that it is with families similar to those in Reid and Shyne's study that social work should be concerning itself, because it is with just such families that social work intervention has a meaningful contribution to make.

It has been suggested that the increased effectiveness of short-term work is a direct result of the greater precision of its objectives and hence the easier it is to measure outcome. Here again, the focus on planned work on specific problems is one of considerable importance to intake workers, who can easily become overwhelmed by the demands made upon them and respond in a piecemeal fashion that has little to do with social work methods. While such responses might serve to resolve the immediate problem or query they do little to help the client as an individual exert control over his own life or enable him to cope more effectively with future problems. Consequently the lessons to be learnt from the study of brief and extended casework carry considerable relevance for local-authority social work practice despite the difference in the clientele served.

Having established both the validity and viability of short-term methods of work in social work settings, there developed a move towards both defining and refining different methods of short-term work. Time-limited work poses problems for agencies which assume responsibility for some forms of long-term case, as is the case with local-authority social services departments, and hence such work is of particular relevance to those teams within such departments which are committed to short-term work – that is, intake teams. Such methods also have practical implications for long-term workers who can easily fall into the compulsive care-giving aspects of traditional social work practice without developing plans, goals, and a focus for work undertaken.

The major development in short-term work has been the growth of task-centred treatment as a short-term model of social work practice designed to alleviate specific problems being experienced by individuals and families. It grew out of Reid and Shyne's work with methods of planned brief treatment and out of work on intervention centred on helping clients define and carry out certain tasks and courses of action. It also clearly has origins in Perlman's formulation of social treatment as a problem-solving process. The model is specifically addressed to the problems of living which a client can, with help, resolve through his own actions. Reid lists the major problem areas amenable to such a method of treatment as: interpersonal conflict, dissatisfaction with social relationships, problems with formal organizations, difficulty in role performance, problems of social transition, reactive emotional distress, and in-adequate resources. Task-centred treatment is highly focused and time limited. Within one or two interviews the worker and the client need to arrive at an explicit agreement on the problems to be dealt with, and the problems defined in terms of specific conditions to be changed.

There is also an agreement on the amount of duration of service, on average six to twelve interviews over two to four months. Ideally

the tasks should be based on what the client thinks would be most
effective in alleviating his problem, and be so structured that the
chances of it being accomplished whole or in part are fairly high.
When this is the case the worker is able to convey realistic, positive
expectations that the client will be successful, and such optimism
and enthusiasm on the part of the worker is likely to contribute to a
successful outcome. The worker's primary role, therefore, is to help
the client formulate target problems and carry out agreed tasks.
This is something of a change from the social worker's traditional
role, for rather than being subtle and implicit, responsive and
indeterminate, the task-centred model requires workers to be
articulate, explicit, and goal orientated. That is, the worker has a
much more active and directive role to play. Task-centred treatment
is thus a highly structured model, utilizing planned brevity, with a
specified treatment focus, an empirical orientation, and emphasis on
client action. However, within the model it can utilize either psychodynamic theory or a more strictly behavioural approach. Reid sees
task-centred theory and practice as bringing together

> 'the more traditional emphasis on the inner man and the newer
> focus on man as doer. . . . Thus the task-centred approach reflects
> two trends: increasing emphasis on action and behaviour as
> treatment foci and, within that development, the push towards
> some synthesis between this newer emphasis and more accepted
> treatment foci on internal processes.'
>
> (Reid 1977: 13)

Once again, this model was developed in the USA and much of
the literature pertains to American practice. Goldberg and Robinson
(1977), however, have specifically tested the model in a local-
authority area-team setting. Commenting that only a small part of a
local-authority social worker's activities can be described as casework, they go on to acknowledge that: 'Social work methods have
not yet been fully adjusted to the changing nature of the local
authority social services, nor has the training of social workers been
sufficiently adapted to meet the changing demands on them'
(Goldberg and Robinson 1977: 243). The introduction and
development of intake teams has aroused interest in expert assessment and short-term work and hence in the task-centred approach.
This approach also addresses itself to the misperceptions of needs

and aims between social workers and clients noted in numerous consumer studies. By virtue of the clear and explicit definition of problems and tasks required in the task-centred approach, such misperceptions should be minimized and clients consequently better able to tackle their problems. Furthermore, the model enhances the respect for the client and stresses his equality as a participating contractor, and it helps to demystify social work by clarifying the worker's role.

The experience of the small sample in the survey undertaken suggested that the model was most successful when applied to problems of inadequate resources. It also looked potentially fruitful in the area of dissatisfaction with social relationships, often found to be related to loneliness and isolation in the elderly or impoverished relationships subsequent to physical or psychological handicaps. However, task-centred work with such clients is also largely dependent on the provision of adequate resources in the community in the form of day centres, clubs, etc., to sustain the initial motivation developed with the social worker.

There emerged two general areas where the task-centred model was not found to be appropriate. The first was in relation to some aspects of agency function; that is, where the surveillance and protective functions of the social services department were paramount. Secondly, some client's problems were not amenable to such an approach, either because the target problem was not acknowledged by the client or not agreed upon between the client and worker, or because no feasible task could be developed. Respondents to the Department of Health and Social Security survey (DHSS 1978) were often found to use the phrase 'task-centred work' loosely, to mean purposeful or planned work, rather than work which had the twin hallmarks of the task-centred method: emphasis on a planned, time-limited approach with clear foci of intervention, and the emphasis on the client's part in resolving his own problems. Task-centred work requires relatively high motivation on the part of the client and it is necessary, given the range of complexity of clients' problems, to develop skills in isolating and selecting appropriate tasks. It was found to be:

'rare at the point of allocation or assessment to think in terms of specific tasks to be completed or to fit problems into broad typologies. Perhaps this could be one way of sharpening diagnostic skills and forging more clear-cut lines between diagnosis and method of intervention.'

(DHSS 1978: 199)

Goldberg suggested that one of the reasons for the limited use of the task-centred method in local-authority social work is the continuing tendency to view the social services department as the last resort when things go wrong; consequently many marital relationships, for example, have broken down irretrievably by the time the client approaches social services, and so what were originally problems of interpersonal conflict are dealt with as problems of social transition or even inadequate resources. Intake workers, therefore, possibly need to seize any opportunity to develop their expertise in this approach, in the expectation that once they can demonstrate competence in work of this type both clients and other agencies might refer cases where meaningful, structured intervention is likely to achieve a successful outcome. To give the time to undertake such work, intake teams need to examine the system of priorities to which they are working and assess the potential of this approach in comparison with others they use in terms of the type of work undertaken. Whatever the difficulties envisaged in developing a task-centred approach as a method of social work practised at intake, with its shift in emphasis from a passive to active role for the worker and its stress on the definition of tasks for the client to pursue, it has tremendous potential as a framework for dealing with many of the problems presented at intake. As Goldberg and Robinson conclude:

'Even within a general social service agency which dispenses many services and has to undertake a good deal of statutory and voluntary surveillance, the task-centred approach has much to offer. It stimulates clarity of thinking, more explicitness about aims and ways of achieving them, and more focused planning of individual cases. It invites greater participation by the client, who is encouraged to accomplish as much as possible by his own efforts: the evidence of the follow-up interviews shows how proud clients are of their achievements. The method discourages aimless "visiting" unnecessary follow-ups, and a kind of vague responsiveness to any problems that might emerge.'

(Goldberg and Robinson 1977: 266)

Intrinsic to all models of short-term work are the elements of planning, definition of goals, mutually agreed foci of work, and the acceptance by the worker of limited goals – that is, it is impossible to do such a complete piece of work that the client will never need to return and will always be able to deal with any problem. As a result of the increasing awareness of, and interest in, short-term models of intervention in social work there has been a tendency for social workers to describe some of the work they are undertaking as 'contract work'.

Surveys have found (DHSS 1978) that respondents' descriptions of the use of contracts falls into three broad categories: denoting that there are planned goals for intervention, with or without explicitly sharing these with the client; to describe the principles and framework governing the work being undertaken; and finally, more specifically, to describe work where there is an explicit agreement between the worker and the client on the target problem, the goals and strategies of social work intervention, and the roles and tasks of the participants. The use of this last definition serves to clarify what is being undertaken and sets out for worker and client what the expectations are, thereby minimizing the misperception that can so often arise in client-worker relationships. Hutton (1977), in developing a model of short-term contract work, comments that social work interventions that are brief, focal, and effective have tended to be seen as illusory, and relates this to the observation that much social work intervention is characterized by compulsive care giving, which reduces a client's autonomy and increases dependency. Social workers have thus traditionally tended to feel compelled to take the troubles of others onto their own shoulders, rather than acknowledge the client's right to accept or refuse help, and intervene to increase the client's autonomy.

The development of short-term models of work, whether biased towards a psychodynamic or behaviourist approach, has shifted the emphasis back to the client's responsibility for his own actions, and his active role in resolving his problems. By a more-focused specification of goals and targets for intervention, social workers are forced to examine more closely what they are doing, in comparison with much work in social services departments where social workers are often found to be either working to vague and global ends, such as 'offering support' or 'doing preventive work', or else become totally absorbed in carrying out practical tasks. As Hutton concludes:

> 'All social workers have to manage themselves; work in all kinds of agencies can be enhanced by "stopping and thinking" instead of rushing into precipitate action. The discipline of finding the minimum that needs to be done by the worker so that the client can have the achievement of doing the rest for himself can be applied in any setting.'
>
> (Hutton 1977: 118)

The relevance of the unitary model

Vickery (1977) sees the history of social work in Britain from the post-war years until 1970 as being characterized by the struggle between the expansion of specialized fields of practice and the drive towards genericism in training. 'Generic' she takes to refer to that common core of knowledge and skills deemed necessary to the practice of social work no matter in what field of practice, in contrast with 'generalist', meaning general purpose. The Seebohm reorganization resulted in British social workers carrying extensive responsibility to deal with an extremely wide range of problems. However, as a result of the traditional social work focus on the individual and the family, workers often had only a limited conceptual and methodological ability to move outside this circumscribed area of work, and hence the effectiveness of their intervention was limited.

The Seebohm Report stressed the hope that the new social services departments would make available a more varied response to client need, and that the repertoire of skills possessed by social workers would be extended to supplement traditional casework methods. Consequently, generic training would, it was hoped, equip social workers to work not only with individuals but also with groups and communities, as appropriate. Generic training was seen as a way of helping workers develop an understanding of the interrelatedness of different methods, thereby facilitating their practice across the wide and varied fields that came under the province of the new generic departments. Throughout the 1960s the limitations of the traditionally separate perspectives of casework,

groupwork, and community work were being recognized and the
need for a more unified perspective was becoming apparent. The
Seebohm reorganization, perhaps unwittingly, gave further impetus
to such a need.

Social workers in the early 1970s were understandably confused
by the opposing forces found within the profession. Workers were,
for example, torn between the conflicting demands of specialist
versus generalist work; casework versus community work; preventive versus statutory work; work with families versus work with
the elderly; and other such divisions. At the same time, dividing
work along these lines had an air of unreality and many workers
were practising in a much more generalist way. Casework, however,
in its broadest sense, remained the prime method of intervention,
grounded as it is in the individualistic tradition of social work
practice. Research continues to suggest that the vast majority of
social workers employed by local authorities do not practise a
generic approach in their methods of intervention. At the same time,
it is noteworthy that little specific attention is accorded to the skills
needed in relation to the advocacy and broker aspects of the social
workers' role:

> 'Interestingly, although our social workers accepted that a con-
> siderable amount of indirect work on behalf of clients (advocating
> and negotiating with other resource giving agencies and pro-
> fessionals, participating in case conferences and court proceed-
> ings, etc.) was a central and essential part of their role, surprisingly
> few referred to the skills required. There seemed to be an assump-
> tion that one relied on "common sense".'
>
> (DHSS 1978: 256)

Arising, therefore, out of the dissatisfaction with the traditional
divisions in social work practice, together with the much broader
range of demands made on social services departments after reorganization, there developed an interest in the unitary model,
originally formulated in the USA by Pincus and Minehan, as a
framework for examining social work practice, and planning intervention. The unitary model shares a number of features with the
short-term models of work, although these do not include duration of
intervention. Both models depend upon an analysis and definition of
problems, establishing a need for change, determining goals, and

agreeing on the strategies for achieving stated goals. Both emphasize the importance of agreement with clients about the problems to be tackled and the remedies available to resolve them. However, whereas short-term work is a social work method, used with individuals and families to help them resolve their difficulties, unitary theory provides a framework within which to view problems.

Short-term work, therefore, tends to retain the individualistic bias of traditional social work practice, while unitary theory is much more broad based. The unitary perspective shifts social work practice from an individualistic practice perspective to an inter-actionalist one and therefore broadens the scope of social work intervention to include public issues as well as private ills. Hence this perspective includes within the scope of a social worker's practice intervention at the level of social policy and social structure as well as at the level of individual functioning. As such it integrates social work practice at a variety of levels within one frame of reference, rather than polarizing different methods of intervention. Using the unitary model there is no reason why a social worker should not undertake group or community work, for their generic training should allow them to intervene as appropriate, or facilitate that intervention by another worker. Just as short-term work serves to shift the focus from a specialist client group focus to a problem focus, so the unitary model constitutes a shift from a method-centred to a problem-centred model of practice.

The dominant form of both organization and practice in local-authority social services departments is what Evans (1978) calls 'case-based'. That is, the client is nearly always the target for intervention, and although it is increasingly recognized that in the course of contact with a client the social worker may have to deal with the context within which the client's problem lie, for example financial or housing difficulties, dealing with such matters is not seen as employing specific social work skills, and the methods literature is conspicuously silent on the subject of how to exert this sort of social influence. The unitary approach, identifying as it does four basic systems in the practice model – the client system, change-agent system, target system, and action system – emphasizes the importance of social-problem definition and the assessment of where, within accessible social systems, intervention is required. The unitary approach thus removes the sole focus from the client's emotional problems, and focuses in addition on problems in social systems. For example, not only the truant and the family but also the curriculum and the school are possible points for intervention. Social workers, therefore, do not only need to develop their skills in individual work with clients but also need to learn how to deal with recalcitrant officials and how to intervene in social systems outside their own. As Olsen concludes, the need to develop a unitary model of practice

'requires all social workers to have sufficient knowledge and skills in order to conceptualize and practice in a holistic and integrated way; to be able to take account of all systems which affect the individual or group; to identify unmet material need, poor service delivery, and inadequate resources; to promote the application of the rich variety of techniques available to social work on a team-work and intra and inter-personal basis, and to contribute to the improvement and further development of social policy.'

(Olsen 1978: 164)

The unitary model, therefore, stresses the need for the worker to be able to assess problems on a broad canvas, to detect the need for intervention outside client systems, and to be an active go-between in mediation between client groups and social institutions. The unitary approach would seem to require of the individual worker a vast range of knowledge and skill, in the same way as the intake worker requires a tremendous breadth of knowledge and expertise to fulfil the intake worker role. In both cases, however, any individual worker could not fulfil all the possible roles that might be expected of him or her. In the intake worker, one of the major skills is assessment and being able to either direct the client towards, or mobilize, those required resources that are not within the worker's repertoire; so with the unitary model the individual practitioner cannot be expected to be competent to intervene in all the social systems in a particular problem, but should have developed the ability to judge what kind of expertise is required, who should be included, and have the capacity to work in collaboration with variously orientated practitioners, consultants, administrators, and para-professionals.

Social workers have long been sensitive to clients' material needs and the provision of community resources but until relatively recently such concerns have not been viewed as the province of professional social work. Debate has raged as to whether material provision should be a function of social work practice, and the provision of community resources has tended to fall outside the brief of the local-authority social worker, unless employed in what is usually a separate and distinct role as community worker. More recently, and especially after the Seebohm reorganization, the role of the social worker as advocate, mediator, and broker has been given more attention. This is particularly so for intake workers, in their frequent role as middlemen. It is a central theme of the unitary approach that social work is at the interface between the person with problems and the social agency that may be able to help. The crucial role of the social worker is seen to lie in linking people with problems to the appropriate helping agencies, and easing the contact with those agencies where clients have some difficulty in receiving the necessary services.

The unitary approach with this emphasis was initially developed in the USA, where the multiplicity of welfare agencies is much more extensive than in Britain, where the Welfare State accounts for a wide range of basic provision. However, even in Britain social workers are increasingly acting as brokers and advocates on behalf of clients to secure timely, relevant, and more complete responses from such agencies as the Department of Health and Social Security, housing departments, and hospitals. The role of the social worker is thus to seek to modify or build new relatioships between people and social institutions. The unitary approach, in contrast to other models, allows for the fact that at a certain point the social worker may decide that his or her concern and energy should be directed towards the service organizations themselves.

The development of the unitary model in Britain can be viewed as a response to the demand for a theoretical model to describe what social workers actually do. Because of its systems orientation it recognizes multiple causality and, therefore, allows for a more holistic assessment. It is generally acknowledged that, particularly in local-authority social services departments, practitioners use 'bits of this and bits of that' theory and method in their practice. This is especially true of intake workers, where the range of different requests, demands, and needs presented is more extensive and comprehensive than at other points in the agency, where there is generally some degree of selectivity. The unitary model is consequently of great value at the point of intake as offering a framework within which to formulate the problems presented, and plan intervention, not solely on an individualistic basis but also taking into account the role of other social systems. Its acknowledged base in reality removes the narrow traditional approach of the method/skill schools and replaces this with the problem presented as the fundamental focus. Having established with the client the problem that is to be the focus for change and agreed on strategies to achieve this goal, the individual intake worker may not possess the requisite skills, for the range of possible roles and skills encompassed by the unitary approach is vast. Consequently the importance of teamwork and the sharing of knowledge, skills, and expertise is at a premium – for just as in the effective functioning of an intake team, the use of the unitary model presupposes that each member contributes to the work of the team, rather than that one worker should implement all the plans. The use of the unitary model – because of the broad canvas against which it plans intervention – therefore has implications for the deployment of staff, the composition of work teams, and the training of social workers.

7
Intake – a new specialism?

Introduction

The establishment of intake teams in social services departments after the Seebohm reorganization has emerged as one of the major new phenomena in social work in the past decade. Seebohm's preference for generic departments designed to offer a social work service across the client groups, coupled with the increased impetus for all social workers to undertake a common training, and specialization in employment ceasing, has been viewed as resulting in the loss of much of the skill, knowledge, and expertise found in the more specialized departments before the Seebohm reorganization. While some welcomed the trend towards genericism, seeing it as a means of overcoming the earlier fragmentation of service, others have viewed it as affecting unfavourably the quality of service available to clients, feeling that social workers who have no specialist training will be able to offer only a limited degree of help to clients.

Consequently some organizations, e.g. MIND, favour the development of specialist electives in the final year of professional training, while others are opposed to any such specialist input at the stage of initial training on the grounds that basic training is primarily designed to equip social workers for work in social services departments, approximately 90 per cent of social workers in Britain being so employed. Intake workers, by virtue of their structural position in the organization of an area team, are generalist in nature. That is, they deal with the whole range of problems and client groups who call upon the services of the department. Before reorganization not only was there specialization in the department in which the worker was employed, but also a distinction between the administering of social services, that is service delivery, and the provision of a professional social work service, primarily casework. Intake workers are in a position to straddle this divide. Consequently, in the early days of intake teams the work they undertook tended to be viewed as of relatively low status. Only gradually – as the implications of the intake model become clearer and intake workers themselves clarified their role within the department and carved out for themselves a particular area of work covering assessment, crisis, and short-term work – did intake come to be valued as a highly skilled service, requiring a particular range of knowledge and expertise.

Furthermore, the establishment of such teams carries with it major implications for the nature of work undertaken by the rest of the area team and facilitates their potential for professional and organizational initiatives. Intake workers, therefore, fall into the classification 'experienced general-purpose social workers' and thus can be seen as constituting a generic specialism after the Seebohm reorganization.

Intake – a generalist service

Local-authority social services departments have bestowed upon them, by virtue of the legislative framework within which they operate, a certain range of powers and duties. These include the provision of material services – for instance, residential accom-modation for various client groups, aids for the elderly and handi-capped, meals on wheels, and car badges for the physically handi-capped – and the provision of a professional social work service to protect, support, advise, and (in the broadest sense) 'treat' or 'help to change' individuals and families with problems. It is, in effect, at the point of intake that theoretically the whole range of social service provision is available to the client. Being in the front line of the organization, intake teams are included in both the administration of social services – the service delivery end of the spectrum – and the provision of a professional social work service for which particular training and skills are required, the less tangible aspect of social work including the utilization of particular skills and expertise to help clients change their behaviour.

Local-authority social workers, therefore, undertake a series of tasks: protecting vulnerable individuals in emergencies; the supervision of those considered to be 'at risk'; the provision of substitute care on a temporary or permanent basis; the provision of practical services; the provision of information and advice; and working with individuals, families, groups, and communities to enable them to realize their potential and foster their independence.

The traditional division in local-authority social work between the service delivery functions and the 'professional' social work functions has been largely reflected in the status and grading of staff filling the different roles. That is, social work assistants have been employed to work with clients where the need has been seen to be the straightforward provision of services, and qualified social workers to deal with more-complex matters, usualy related to work with families, children, and the mentally ill. This division has tended to develop in such a way that social work assistants deal primarily with elderly and physically handicapped clients, and social workers with all others. The inherent danger of such a situation is that categorization by client group becomes the dominant focus and work is allocated on this basis.

If, therefore, social work assistants are expected to deal with the service delivery end of the social work spectrum, and with the elderly and handicapped, the implication becomes that the elderly and handicapped have a particular range of needs focused on the provision of practical services. Services then tend to be offered by client-group categorization and standardized solutions develop. For example, the standard range of services available to the elderly – home help, luncheon clubs, meals on wheels, district nurse, day care, warden-supervised accommodation, and residential care – can become 'pre-packed' service packages for the elderly, the services in the package depending on the degree of physical/mental deterioration a particular client suffers.

Whilst it is indisputable that this group of clients require practical services, there is a danger of overlooking the human, emotional problems they might be experiencing by categorizing the client as elderly and, therefore, in need of one or more of a particular range of predetermined services. There is an unfortunate tendency for work

,with the elderly and handicapped to be generally viewed as relatively routine and mundane, and thus not to attract the interest of the majority of qualified staff. In the study of Social Services Teams (DHSS 1978) work with the elderly was found to be relatively 'unpopular' with social work students. While 88 per cent of the sample of students said they would like to work with families and children, only 28 per cent said this of work with the elderly. In addition, the priority given to, and pressure of, statutory child-care work invariably results in most qualified social workers carrying case-loads biased in this direction. Consequently many of the less tangible and practical problems of the elderly remain unsolved.

While new work is referred as through, for example, a duty system where relatively little initial information is required, or where duty work is perceived as little more than a clerical function of recording the basic details of the client – name, address, age, etc. – and the nature of the request, categorization by client group will probably be perpetuated. In such a system work is allocated with comparatively little initial information and the tendency must be to allocate by client group – that is, certain groups will be allocated to social work assistants, the implication being that the client's needs are for practical services. This means that certain grades of worker effectively specialize in dealing with different client groups, particularly social work assistants with the elderly, and that because of the traditional expectations that social work assistants are primarily concerned with the provision of straightforward, practical services, these are the prime needs of the elderly. This is not to suggest that social work assistants are not often highly sensitive and perceptive workers who undertake a much wider brief than this in their work with clients, but it does serve to highlight the advantages of a system of organization whereby adequate initial assessment is a built-in feature.

Intake teams, because they deal with the whole range of initial requests, provide the whole spectrum of services that the department offers, both practical and non-practical. If the team consists of qualified and experienced staff the question then often arises as to the value of having such staff deal with straightforward and routine requests. If a certain range of such tasks is undertaken by a particular grade of worker, then it can be argued that the use of qualified staff to handle these requests is a waste of a scarce resource. However, to try to divide up the range of requests made at the point of initial contact and have qualified intake workers deal only with a proportion of these – namely, more-complex matters relating to families, children, and mental health – while other requests are directed towards social work assistants (namely, those relating to the elderly), requires that someone is in the position to make these initial decisions. Realistically, this could be done only on the basis of the client group the referral related to, or the nature of the request.

If such a system were in operation the premature categorization of referrals would result, at times, in inappropriate allocation. Such a system would further perpetuate the already implicit assumption that certain client groups need only a certain range of services, and contribute to the criticisms that intake teams tend to deal only with presenting problems. Inherent in the use of certain grades of worker with particular client groups is a denial of the emotional and relationship problems of those client groups dealt with by social work assistants. A request from an elderly person for a particular service may mask a much more complex emotional problem. For example, an elderly couple in their eighties are referred as wanting to apply for warden-supervised accommodation, although both are fairly healthy and occupying pleasant ground-floor owner-occupied accommodation. On this basis an application is made but not granted high priority in the light of available resources.

This request, however, was not caused by accommodation need but rather by the fact that a relative who had occupied the upstairs of the property for many years had recently died. This relative had always taken care of all the financial and business matters for himself and the couple downstairs, with whom he had been heavily involved. His death threw the elderly couple back on each other in a way they had never had to cope with throughout their marriage, in addition to leaving them to manage all financial and business transactions, which they had never done. Their resulting panic caused them to seek a change of accommodation as a solution to their difficulties, both emotional and practical. Such a referral highlights the dangers of viewing service delivery requests from the elderly at face value. Of course, many such requests are just that – a need for a particular service. The value, therefore, of experienced and qualified workers in intake teams is to form an initial assessment as to the client's situation and needs, the work thereafter being allocated as is deemed appropriate. As such, requests assessed to be for a straightforward service, if they cannot be dealt with on the spot, can be allocated to and followed up by a social work assistant working with the intake team.

The British Association of Social Workers' report on the Social Work Task suggests that the role of 'diagnostician', 'which is particularly important at the initial stage of social work intervention and which involves discussing and identifying with clients the nature of the referral' should 'normally only be performed by an appropriately qualified social worker' (BASW 1977: 5: 9).

Intake workers are, therefore, at the interface between the service delivery and traditional professional social work practice ends of the local-authority social services spectrum. They are generic workers not only in terms of covering a range of client groups but also in offering a wide variety of services, skills, knowledge, and expertise. The prime task of an intake worker must be to undertake adequate assessments of client need using a range of social work skills, whatever the apparent simplicity or complexity of the referral. Only on the basis of such initial assessments can any decisions be made about initial short-term and longer term management of the case. Because, therefore, of the range of problems presented at intake an intake team, to function effectively, requires that workers share a common base level of skills and competence. That is, intake workers must be able to work at a competent level across the whole range of problems and client groups, but not necessarily at a specialist level in any one of them.

Variables affecting transfer from intake

For intake teams to function adequately and in accordance with the objectives for which they were originally established, it is important that the variables that come into play in decision making at the next stage are clearly understood. That is, what happens to cases once referred to intake, whether further work is undertaken, and if so by whom. Intake teams are, ideally, able to absorb the area's referrals in making initial assessments of new cases. However, unless there is some flow of work from intake to other teams or agencies the system becomes saturated and rapidly ceases to fulfil its original functions of providing an efficient and effective service that can respond rapidly to requests for help. Whereas in long-term teams the closure of cases tends to be related to the acceptance of new ones – when a case is closed the worker has the time to take on another – no such system operates for intake workers. In intake teams, the continuous pressure of new referrals affects the decisions that are made about existing intake cases as well as affecting the response to new referrals.

Because of the 'one door' for all referrals and because social services departments do not deny access to clients, the demands made upon intake workers cannot be mediated in the same way as those made on long-term workers. Intake workers are, therefore, under constant pressure to take referrals, and it is in the area of subsequent action that decision making becomes the crucial element.

In an ideal model, decision making would focus primarily on two points. Firstly, at the time of referral, a decision on whether the problem, as assessed by the intake worker, is appropriate to the agency; if so, whether it is likely that social work input will be of assistance; and if this is believed to be so, whether the case is more appropriately dealt with on a short-term basis by an intake worker, or should be transferred to a long-term worker. Secondly, it may be the case that after a period of work undertaken by the intake worker the client's difficulties are not resolved and the case may at that point be assessed to need long-term work and, therefore, transferred. There are also those cases where action has to be taken in an emergency and because of the remit of intake teams and their comparative flexibility they work with the case initially – despite its apparent long-term nature – until it can be appropriately trans-ferred to a long-term worker.

However, this model presupposes an uninterrupted flow of work through the area team – that is, that both long-term and intake workers are readily available to accept new cases and consequently that decisions are made solely on the basis of professional social work assessment. In reality staffing levels are invariably thought to fall short of client need, which therefore affects decision making at both the initial referral stage and the subsequent post-intake stage. Sainsbury and Nixon (1979) found that in the local-authority social work cases studied, 52 per cent of clients and social workers in 80 per

cent of cases felt that the services offered could have been better, yet
insufficient agency resources were mentioned in only 23 per cent of
cases. Clients and social workers felt that inadequate time, inadequate skills, and inappropriate attitudes on the part of the
worker were more significant factors.

There usually exists a range of options as to how the case in any
particular referral may be allocated and what work undertaken. It is
at this point that departmental, area, and team decisions on
priorities become pertinent. There exists, either explicitly or implicitly, a hierarchy of need in accordance with which work is
allocated. Individuals deemed 'at risk' are invariably afforded the
highest priority, and referrals in this category are seen as requiring
immediate attention. Even within this high-priority category, there
is a variation in response, with children at risk ranking highest, in
the light of media criticism, followed by the vulnerable elderly and
then other adults, particularly the mentally ill and mentally handicapped. After intake assessment, therefore, certain types of cases
have to be allocated: those of individuals at risk; requests for services
which would not be dealt with at the initial interview; requests for
residential accommodation; and requests for investigation, assessment, or both from other professionals or third parties. The resulting
allocation of work comprises an intricate balancing act, and because
intake teams comprise only one variable within an area team, the
structure and ethos of the whole area team is central to questions of
allocation and the flow of work through the team. Without an
overview of how the area team functions as a whole, an intake team
is doomed as it is in danger of becoming saturated by new cases
because it is unable to assess the feasibility of accepting certain areas
of work, where the department has a choice as to whether to
undertake work or whether to pursue a certain case further once
accepted.

Within an area team, organizational factors such as the availability and deployment of resources – particularly staff and the use
the team makes of such staff as social work assistants, clerical staff,
volunteers, and specialist workers – all have a major effect on the
decisions taken as to whether and how cases will be worked with.
The grading, training, aptitude, and interests of individual workers
exert a major influence on the service available to clients and
thereby affect the general ethos of the team. The quality and

quantity of supervision available to staff serves to mobilize and facilitate individual worker's, and hence the team's, functioning.

The prime resources available to an area team are its staff and their skills. Decisions about the allocation of work have to be taken in the light of the skills available. In cases where there is a clear statutory responsibility the question of allocation rests on which staff have both the experience and time to be able to accept it. However, there are a large number of cases presented at intake where the acceptance or otherwise for social work is less clear cut and while ideally the case would be allocated, the shortage of suitable staff creates a problem. It is in this area that intake teams run the risk of becoming overloaded. The deployment of staff between intake and long-term teams depends largely on the profile of the area served. Where there are high numbers of children in care there is a consequent need for adequately staffed long-term teams to carry such cases. If, however, long-term workers carry fairly static case-loads, then their ability to accept new cases awaiting transfer from intake is minimal and intake workers become overburdened.

Decision making within the intake team is, therefore, coloured by their knowledge about the possibility of the long-term teams accepting cases. Consider an area team comprising an intake team and two long-term geographically based teams, A and B. If one of the long-term teams, A, is short staffed this will affect the work of the intake team and ultimately affect the service offered to new clients from A and B. Because certain high-priority cases have to be dealt with, notably children at risk, intake workers have to respond immediately to referrals falling into this category. If there are a number of new referrals of children at risk in area A, intake respond and after assessment several families need intensive long-term support either to prevent a child coming into care or because the child is in care as a result of the referral, these cases are carried by the intake workers. Because team A is short staffed there is no likelihood of the cases being transferred in the near future; consequently, the intake workers will have to carry these in addition to their own short-term and intake-duty work.

Although team B is adequately staffed and able to take new work the pressures on intake created by A's lack of staff result in either cases being passed inappropriately to B because intake are under such pressure they are not carrying out adequate assessments, or cases which would benefit from long-term social work are not passed through, also because of inadequate assessments. Intake cannot continue to function if they are unable to pass work through to A, and become overloaded. In such a situation, because they cannot actually mediate the initial demands made upon them, the likelihood is that they may look to their own short-term cases and close those prematurely, or else give only the most perfunctory service to new referrals, concentrating exclusively on the resolution of the presenting problems. In addition, intake workers may react by referring work – which they would in less-demanding circumstances have accepted – to other agencies, particularly those areas of work where there is a substantial overlap with other agencies such as the Citizens Advice Bureaux, as is the case in referrals relating to fuel disconnections, welfare-rights advocacy, and semi-legal advice functions. Areas of work such as this may or may not be more appropriately dealt with by social services or another agency, but the former are in a better position to assess the wider dimensions of the problem than that presented and hence to offer a degree of preventive input, for example the possibility of a day-nursery place for a single parent experiencing financial difficulties and becoming depressed at being alone in her home with her young children, or suggestions about mother and toddler groups to help alleviate her isolation.

The work of an intake team and the decisions about how work is allocated in the light of a range of options, is, therefore, inextricably interwoven with the level of functioning of the whole area team. Where there are workers in long-term teams particularly interested or experienced in particular areas of work – for example, working with adolescents, the mentally ill, or mentally handicapped – this is likely to influence the response of intake workers to such referrals.

In cases where intake workers may not consider that they are able, given their remit to deal with short-term work, to offer a service, and where the option would be to deal with the immediate problem and then close the case, the presence of workers in long-term teams with particular interests extends the range of options and provides the opportunity for work of a more preventive nature to be undertaken. It is, therefore, the skills of the whole team that influence the course of any particular case.

The implications of intake for long-term work

Where the model of organization utilized by an area team is one of an intake team feeding work through to long-term teams, there exist substantial differences in the nature of the work and hence the social work practice found in the intake and long-term teams. The types of cases taken on by long-term workers are, by definition, of a long-term or chronic nature and comprise primarily work with children – either on a statutory basis because the children are in care or on supervision to the local authority, or work with families aimed at preventing the necessity of children coming into care – and work with vulnerable 'at-risk' adults from other client groups, including the elderly, physically handicapped, and mentally ill. Long-term teams are wholly dependent on the intake team for the work which they take on. Because intake workers control the flow of work both into the area team and between intake and long-term teams by virtue of their position in the organizational structure, the question arises as to how much influence long-term workers are able to exercise over the criteria used by intake for the acceptance or rejection of cases. Where there is little communication between intake and long-term teams at either fieldworker or team-leader level, there is an inherent danger that intake workers will assess cases as needing long-term social work with little or no reference to the interests, aptitude, or spare time available in the long-term team to accept the case to the advantage of the client.

In addition, the rate of closure of cases by long-term workers is directly related to their ability to take on new work. Consequently, long-term work needs to be constantly reviewed in the light of the progress being made on any particular case. Where there is little feedback between the teams, intake workers may accept cases deemed as unsuitable or inappropriate by long-term workers, with consequent deleterious effects on the transfer process, long-term workers either refusing to accept such cases or only doing so unwillingly, probably resulting in the client receiving a less than adequate service. Also, where communication between the teams is minimal there is little incentive for long-term workers to close cases. At the extreme this lack of communication between intake and long-term teams can result in the area team consisting apparently of several separate teams running along parallel lines.

It is, therefore, imperative that the area team as a whole develop some consensus on what sorts of cases it is felt appropriate for the area team to accept, and the priority of these different areas of work. This then provides a framework within which both intake and long-term teams operate and enables them to function in a complentary manner. As a result of the political pressure that generally prevails to afford high priority to cases including children 'at risk', other client groups, notably the mentally handicapped, chronically mentally ill, and the disabled, are classified as lower priority and are, therefore, likely to receive only a crisis service from intake teams rather than being allocated to a long-term worker. The knowledge in intake teams that particular long-term workers are interested in particular client groups affects the way in which intake workers perceive such cases in that it opens up an avenue for work including more than the presenting problem, and the possibility of transfer to a long-term worker.

Pressure on long-term workers comes presumably from two directions: pressure as a result of crises in their own cases, and pressure caused from the requests from intake workers that they accept new work. The former cannot be mediated and the worker, therefore, has to work with these cases as seems appropriate. Long-term workers can, however, mediate the pressures from intake workers by asserting that they are unable to accept any further work in the light of their existing commitments. If this is agreed by the team leader, intake teams are left holding the case pending transfer. Alternatively, the case may be held by long-term teams pending allocation. Whichever is the case, it is necessary for both teams to have an understanding of where responsibility for such cases lies to prevent protracted negotiation and conflict when some action has to be taken such as in an emergency, and both teams deny responsibility. The capacity of long-term teams is consequently a major influence on intake in relation to what cases are accepted by intake workers and on what basis.

For example, when the long-term teams are stretched it is likely that intake workers are likewise under pressure because of the difficulties of transferring work and hence, as intake workers know that certain types of cases will have to be allocated to long-term workers, especially children in care, this will affect the intake workers' response to other clients where ideally long-term work would be seen as appropriate – for example, a referral of a child newly diagnosed as handicapped, or a chronically mentally ill son and his mother experiencing difficulties. In the previous section, the tendency for intake workers to close, sometimes prematurely, their short-term cases to accommodate the bombardment with new referrals was discussed. Intake teams, therefore, can be seen to adapt their work loads and styles of intervention in the light of the prevailing demands being made upon them and the capacity of workers in other teams to accept work.

Gostick (1976) argues that there is thus a tendency for intake teams to become insular and self-contained, because after their establishment in the early 1970s such teams demonstrated their initial organizational effectiveness by containing the increasing referral rates and hence protecting long-term workers from experiencing the full force of the demands being made. The effectiveness of intake teams in administratively handling the high referral rates was recognized, and more social work resources were channelled into intake, the number of workers in such teams tending to increase, and intake team leaders becoming recognized posts. Gostick believed that the increased size of intake teams fostered the development of an aura of élitism, resulting in their separating themselves from the rest of the team's work. If this becomes the case then there is a danger of communication with long-term teams breaking down. Whilst hypothetically this is possible, it is clear that an area-team model of organization that incorporates intake and long-term teams takes account of the interrelatedness of these two areas of work for which the department is responsible, and that while there are differences in the nature of the work undertaken in these teams, there is also a continuum in some cases between them, meaning that for the model to function adequately the internal channels of communication must be open.

Significantly, in a survey of intake teams recently undertaken by Gostick and Scott (1980) of 15 English local authorities, comprising 129 area teams of which 60 had intake teams, the intake teams were evenly divided on the question of whether transfer was seen as problematic. Very few replies referred to the existence of agreed policy and criteria for case transfer, the decision about transfer lying variously with the intake worker, intake-team leader, and long-term team leader, or some combination of the three. The major problems specified in case transfer were related to reallocation rather than the principle of whether or not certain cases should be transferred. It would, therefore, seem that while the transfer of cases may well be problematic in relation to the availability of suitable staff to take cases, it is not the case that the problems are such that they render the model dysfunctional.

Long-term work differs from that in intake in that it does not incorporate the breadth of advisory and advocacy functions, nor straight service delivery elements, that are found at intake. This is not to say that such elements do not feature in long-term work, but where they do it is likely to be in the context of other long-term problems which are the major focus for work undertaken. The relationship the worker develops with the client is generally of greater significance in long-term cases, and while elements of short-term, task-centred, and contract work can be put to good use in work with long-term clients, this is undertaken against the background of the continuing worker-client relationship.

In theory, the fact that intake workers function to relieve the extraneous pressure of new referrals on long-term workers should serve not only to improve the quality of long-term work and reduce caseload size, but also to allow long-term workers to undertake more preventive and innovative types of work, on an individual or group basis, and to develop special interests and aptitudes. In long-term teams there is much greater scope for worker preference to play a part in staff deployment and the development of expertise. Because at the point of long-term allocation there is a degree of choice between workers which rarely exists at intake, it is both possible and feasible for workers to specialize in work with particular client groups or social work methods. That is, in long-term teams there is the opportunity for specialization in terms of its traditional meaning in social work – workers may choose to specialize in working with a particular group such as the mentally ill, work with under fives, work with adolescents, or in the use of a particular social work method such as family therapy, groupwork, or individual casework. In long-term teams, therefore, it is possible to develop the concept of a generic team, comprising a number of specialist-orientated workers. Such specialists are then in a position to act as a resource of knowledge, expertise, and skills for all the other staff in the area.

An alternative which seems to be gaining ground in some local authorities recently is the establishment of specialist long-term teams, such that a generic intake team feeds work through to a number of long-term teams organized not on the basis of the geographical patch but on the client group served. The intake team would then communicate with a series of teams who worked with the elderly, the mentally ill, adolescents, under fives, etc. In some ways such a model is vaguely reminiscent of the pre-Seebohm classifications, carrying with it the inherent danger of buck-passing caused by dispute on the nature of the 'real' problem and hence which team should accept it. The development of such specialized teams is undoubtedly a reaction to the loss of specialist skills and knowledge in the generic 'boom' after the Seebohm reorganization, and the feeling that the service to clients has suffered as the result of the loss of expertise. This development, currently in its infancy, highlights the differences in nature between intake and long-term work.

In terms of professional social work practice, in an intake/long-term model of area-team organization, intake workers have the advantage of being at the point where the client first presents with a problem, and of undertaking the initial assessment. This point therefore acts as a particular focus for social work intervention even in those cases where the social work function is of a protective or investigatory nature rather than at the voluntary request of the client. Practice theories can thus be related directly to the problem at hand. Sainsbury and Nixon's study (1979) of long-term family casework in social services, probation, and Family Service Units found that there was little serious discrepancy at the beginning of work undertaken between the perspectives of workers and those of clients on the areas of clients' functioning on which it would be desirable to seek some change. In approximately 60 per cent of cases the goals of clients and workers were the same. In the other 40 per cent discrepancies were related to an extension of purpose on the part of the workers, undisclosed to clients. Typically this included an aspiration on the part of the worker to improve family relationships while explicitly working on, perhaps, financial problems.

Consequently at the initial stages of social work intervention aims and purposes were clear to all parties, but as time went on an air of mystification of clients was detected, related to the undisclosed aims of the worker. Some workers were found to lack a consistent practice, thereby causing work undertaken – from the perspective of the participants – to be perceived as aimless, muddled, and even deleterious to morale. Short-term changes were achieved in response to crises but in relatively few cases did clients or workers feel that consistent and planned social work intervention had served to change events and circumstances in the long-term. One of the reasons for this was seen to be that social workers tended to define their work in terms of support and advocacy, rather than in relation to 'training' their clients in the social skills required in dealing with the plethora of social agencies they would have to approach. Consequently, clients remain dependent on their social workers, particularly at times of crisis, and the longer term goals of enabling clients to become self-sufficient are not realized.

This study shows that intake workers are, in fact, in a prime position in dealing with problems at the point where they present a crisis to the client and that it is at this time that much of the most useful work is done. The benefit of social work intervention in the longer term with many cases is questionable when taken in the light of the comments offered by clients, and it is salutory to note the number of cases on long-term workers' caseloads which are closed when the worker leaves, which begs the question of why such cases have been held open.

Long-term work can thus be seen to vary significantly from intake work in various ways. Long-term teams tend to lack integration because they do not, on the whole, function together as a team to handle new work. Much work remains on an individual case basis, little use being made of the expertise or strengths of other team members, leaving the client wholly dependent on the limited expertise and vision of the individual worker. As a result the work satisfaction and morale of long-term workers does not have the same shared focus as in intake teams, where group cohesion and mutual support is generally high. However, developments in the organiz-ation of long-term work either as increasing patch orientation or as the emergence of specialist teams is likely to provide a more tangible focus and point of identification for such workers, who may seek to cement their group identity by working jointly in areas or particular projects related to either the needs of their patch or of the particular client group served. Because of the symbiotic relationship of intake and long-term teams, the strengthening of the latter could well be advantageous to the functioning of the area team as a whole.

Intake and specialization

Before the Seebohm reorganization, most practising social workers were not professionally trained, their skills and expertize resting on their work experience, which was invariably of a particular type of work, owing to the organizational structure of the personal social services. Furthermore, although many training courses claimed to be generic in design and content, most social workers who did go on training courses did so with the explicit expectation of returning to work in a particular department, that is, an agency that specialized on the basis of client group served. Consequently, workers developed a relatively high degree of specialization at an early stage in their career, resulting in the differentiation in title, status, and salary scale of workers, and fostering dissatisfaction amongst staff who were essentially undertaking tasks of a similar nature contributing to the general welfare of the family.

What was suggested to the Seebohm Committee to overcome the confusion caused by the existing service pattern was that 'An all-purpose social welfare service could act as a clearing house in this respect and refer cases to the appropriate social worker' (HMSO 1968: paragraph 510). Whereas this 'clearing-house' function was not an appropriate one for the new departments as a whole, the development of intake teams can be seen as in many ways a direct response to just the kind of confusion that gave rise to this suggestion. Intake teams, generic in practice by their very location and function, do indeed function to some extent as a clearing house, referring clients where appropriate to either different agencies or other workers in the same agency. It is, however, this same function that has tended, particularly in the early days of the development of such teams, to cause them to be viewed as low status, undertaking unskilled tasks; in some cases little more than a clerical/reception function. Once intake teams became more established in themselves and clear about their role within their own agency, then the range of knowledge, skills, and expertise required of the workers became clearer, and such teams generally expanded to work not solely as a clearing house referring clients elsewhere, but also to deal with assessment, crisis, and short-term work and there was a consequent shift towards acknowledging the high level of skill and expertise required in such work. As such, however, they have served to act as a focal point for referrals both from the general public and from other referral agents with the object of providing a more consistent service.

Social workers in the unified departments were to be expected to work across traditional client-group divisions. The newly qualified worker entering the department was expected to initially carry a limited work load but to rapidly develop the ability to undertake a wide range of social work functions. Whilst the development of special interests was acknowledged as a possibility, the pursuance of these on the part of the worker was possible only so far as it did not conflict with other agency and client needs. Specialization was viewed as necessary above basic-grade level to facilitate the advancement of knowledge and to give a consultant capacity to staff within the department.

Seebohm's recommendations on the structure of the new social services departments and on the role of specialization had clear implications for the direction of social work training. Staff required training in the principles and skills that are common to all forms of social work with individuals and families. In addition, work with groups and communities was seen as an integral part of the new department's work load and consequently staff needed training in these areas too. The view was taken that the common elements in the practice of social work in different settings are more important than the elements which distinguish them, and hence these common core elements should provide the basis of qualification courses. It was acknowledged that there would be a need for staff with special interests and expertise and, it was suggested, in many instances further training to act as specialist advisers and consultants at headquarters level, and perhaps in area teams as well. The expectation was that as the service developed specialisms would cluster differently and new types of specialism would emerge to meet new problems.

The role of specialist workers in social services departments has so far proved a relatively uneasy one. The tendency to base specialist staff centrally has resulted in confusion of their role on the part of area-team staff, in addition to suspicion of their role as 'outsiders'.

Furthermore, such workers are often difficult to accommodate within the local authorities' sacred cow of line management, and consequently are left somewhat in limbo as advisers and consultants but with little structural power with which to develop their role and influence other staff in the department. In terms of the development of new specialisms as a result of reorganization it is arguable that one such specialism, although not in the traditional meaning, is that of intake work. Also, intake work is the most generic work under-taken in area teams, as a result of its location and function within the agency. Seebohm's conception of a basic-grade worker in a social services department is:

'The kind of social worker we expect to emerge will be one who has had a generic training specially aimed at giving him competence, after experience, to cope with a whole range of social need, provided he has the support of adequate consultation and other resources' (HMSO 1968: paragraph 527).

Specialization can be viewed in two different ways. Firstly, it can be viewed as a horizontal division between different methods of work and the extent to which work with different client groups creates a particular specialism, somewhat like the case of the different depart-ments before the Seebohm reorganization. Alternatively, specializ-ation may be used to mean a qualitative difference in the degree of skill a social worker possesses; that is, it may be regarded as a vertical division of the department's staff structure. Bromley (1978), focusing on the vertical dimension of specialization, distinguishes between 'concentration' and 'expertise'. 'Concentration' he takes to be the propensity for a social worker to undertake a limited number of different types of case or task, which do not require any distinctive practice competence or expertise. 'Expertise', on the other hand, he views as developed at a later stage in the individual worker's career when he acquires an internalization of knowledge and an integration of this with practice experience such that a distinctive practice competence or expertise is developed.

However, even given this clarification the basis for the specialism/ expertise remains unclear. It is generally seen by practitioners as referring to work with a particular client group or method of working. That is, most social workers returning to a local authority social services department after training will not initially be placed in a situation where specialization is in terms of horizontal divisions (although there are exceptions where departments have, for example, specialist fostering and adoption or housing social work sections which accept newly qualified workers). Rather, they are likely to work as basic-grade generic workers and only at a later stage, if at all, develop skill and expertise in a particular area of work. Less usually the location of work may provide the foundation for such expertise. It is because intake work does not clearly fall into the traditional client-group/method of work pattern that it has tended not to be viewed as a specialist area of work, albeit one nevertheless requiring a high degree of skill and expertise. The determining factor in the nature and content of intake work is its function and location within the agency – as a front-line organization performing a gatekeeper role for both the department and other agencies, and providing an assessment, crisis, and short-term service. Intake workers are not generally able to concentrate on a limited number of different types of case or task but rather develop skill in a wide range of work, covering many client groups and different methods of intervention.

Intake work, therefore, can be viewed as a specialist area of work by virtue of its location, and based on the wide range of knowledge required and the range of methods and models of intervention used. As a result of the pressure arising out of the location of work, assessment skills and the use of short-term models of intervention can be seen as the hallmarks of 'specialist' intake workers. Taking Bromley's view that expertise at an advanced stage means the development of distinctive practice competence, then intake work can be viewed as a specialism in itself. The term 'specialist', therefore, can be used to denote a worker of distinctive practice competence, whether working generically or in a narrowly defined field of practice.

Having established that social work training in Britain should be generalist in orientation to prepare students to return to work, on the whole, in generic departments, and that the expected pattern is that any specialist skills and expertise will be developed at a post-basic-grade level, the question then arises as to how this is to be done. Vickery (1973), while acknowledging that all social workers need to maintain a very broad diagnostic sensitivity to be able to differentiate what they can deal with and what is more appropriately referred elsewhere, argues that there is 'general-purpose social work' on the one hand and 'specialization' at an advanced level on the other. Further:

> 'Unless or until social workers deepen their knowledge and skills in particular problem areas and types of social work intervention the ability of agencies to offer more than a limited degree of help will be in serious doubt no matter how wide the range of problems with which theoretically they are supposed to deal.'
>
> (Vickery 1973: 262)

The solution to this has been seen to lie in the development of post-qualification courses to enable experienced practitioners to consolidate and develop their knowledge and skills in particular areas. Such post-qualification training could also serve to bring qualified workers up to date with the new models and methods of professional practice. However, while basic training has forged ahead over the past decade, the post-qualification programme has stumbled. In 1977 there were 153 places on 24 post-qualification courses, and although the number of courses has now increased to about thirty, employers still see such courses as very much the frills on the cake of basic training, the latter being given priority over the former. This tendency is reinforced by the career structure in social services departments where supervisory and management skills are what are rewarded, and career advancement is largely dependent on a generalist perspective. As a result only those with limited career aspirations tend to be attracted to single-subject specialisms. For example, a course for specialist workers for the blind and deaf could not attract sufficient students because students did not want to be typecast, since this would, in their eyes, reduce their subsequent career opportunities.

Consequently, generic basic training is ideally followed by specialist post-qualification training opportunities, but this in reality is not so, and the vast majority of workers have no further formal training after their basic-qualification courses. Specialization as such, therefore, whether by client group, method of work, or location of work, arises primarily out of direct work experience, and is consolidated by the efforts of the individual rather than any structure for professional development.

The British Association of Social Workers, in a paper on the Social Work Task published in 1977, comment that developments in social work education have stressed the shared values and common elements in social work whatever the setting or circumstances, resulting in the view that the same social worker ought to be able to deal with all members of a family no matter how different their problems. Social workers in social services departments, as a result of the trend advocated by Seebohm towards genericism in both training and practice, are seen by the authors of the paper to respond now to a much wider range of problems but to do so on a more superficial level.

Consequently they favour a move back towards specialization on the following grounds: the increased range and volume of work undertaken by social services departments requires examination of the deployment of staff; the development of social work theory and expanding fields of knowledge are such that no individual can be expected to incorporate all; if knowledge of a particular area of work is to be used and developed, then it is necessary to limit the range of work the individual worker undertakes; the development of expertise requires particular individuals to possess the knowledge and skills to help less-experienced colleagues with complex problems; individual workers have different motivations and preferences and to deny these lowers morale and, therefore, practice standards; and finally, social workers are better at some areas of work than others. The development of social work as a profession they view as closely related to the growth of specialization. The implications of this for training follow the standard line of a broad, general training to provide individuals with a sound base on which to decide about subsequent specialization, and to prevent the blinkered approach associated with premature specialization. Post-qualification training would be the means of specializing, and such specialist staff would then be available to advise general-purpose social workers.

Newly qualified social workers would, therefore, work as generalists, perhaps developing some special interest. Above this there would be specialists with post-qualification training working with particular client groups; methods of intervention; or else in fields of planning, management, or policy development. That is, the current practice whereby promotion above basic-grade level almost invariably implies a move into some sort of managerial post would be changed and there would be a possibility of retaining experienced and committed fieldworkers as practitioners rather than losing them to management. Finally, however, in addition to basic-grade generalist workers and specialist workers, there are those staff who do not wish to pursue any specialist training in relation to particular client groups or methodology, yet who possess considerable experience in 'general-purpose' social work, and a wide knowledge of how to help with a range of problems, linked with assessment skills on referral to more specialist workers or agencies.

Much of the assessment and short-term work undertaken by intake workers falls to this latter group of 'experienced general-purpose social workers', who become specialists in this aspect of social work by virtue of their experience and skills. This does not mean that they do not require post-qualification training to enable them to better fulfil their role; but rather the nature and content of such training is likely to be different to that of other specialist training, concentrating on methods of intervention that can be applied across a wide range of problem areas and client groups. These include task-centred work or crisis intervention, and the acquisition and development of knowledge in such areas as law and welfare rights to assist workers in their advocacy and information-giving functions. Also, at intake more than at any other point in social services departments it is important to have a firm grasp of the role and function of other agencies and professionals at both a local and national level.

Interestingly, despite the widely acknowledged necessity to divide work in such a way as to make areas manageable for individual workers, the Department of Health and Social Security research into social services teams found, in examining the role of specialization: 'What is striking, however, is how little attempt has been made to divide up work, except in relation to problems of intake' (DHSS 1978: 102). Therefore, the only 'new specialism' to have developed at all widely, ten years after the Seebohm reorganization, is apparently that of the experienced general-purpose intake worker. This is particularly because of the paucity of post-qualification courses and the commitment to generic basic training.

Conclusions

All agencies have to devise procedures whereby incoming work is handled. Given this, the issue becomes one of organizing in such a way that the system devised operates to the advantage of both the agency and the consumers. Intake teams were developed as a means of handling the vast diversity of work that flooded into the newly established area teams after the Seebohm reorganization. The existence of a particular team with a remit to deal with all new work, whether on an assessment, crisis or short-term basis, was seen as constituting a rational deployment of area-team resources.

Wetton (1976), in an evaluative study of an intake team set up in Cheltenham in 1974, lists five major aims articulated at its inception. These represent the common themes running through the reasoning behind the setting up of most such teams. The establishment of an intake/long-term model of organization within an area team was seen as: facilitating a more rapid response to requests for help; increasing expertise in effective assessment, crisis, and short-term work; allowing long-term workers to plan their work more effectively; encouraging realistic caseload management; and freeing long-term workers to enable them to provide a real rehabilitative and preventive service to families. The realization of these aims was viewed as a way of increasing workers' job satisfaction, whether in intake or long-term teams. There is little dispute that the aims set out above are largely achieved by effective intake-team organization.

Gostick (1976), however, argues that it may be the case that intake teams contain the seeds of their own destruction. Initially set up to facilitate the work of the whole area team, in the early 1970s most intake teams were relatively small in terms of numbers of social workers and often shared a team leader with another team. As they demonstrated their initial organizational effectiveness by coping with the growing referral rates of the time, more social work services were channelled into intake teams such that the teams became larger, commonly with their own team leaders. There then arose the danger that intake teams would develop an élitism that separated them from the rest of the area team, causing them to become insular and self-contained, resulting in a breakdown of communication with the long-term teams, little work being passed on, and intake becoming saturated. Clearly, if an impasse such as this is reached the model is no longer workable. To function effectively it requires an area commitment, and open communication between teams.

In addition to the avowed objectives in the establishment of intake teams, the model based on an intake/long-term division also serves to highlight inherent pitfalls, and to render secondary gains. Intake workers have to remain alert to the possibility of prematurely categorizing problems to make sense, to themselves, of the chaos with which they are confronted. There is a tendency to rework problems as presented so that they fit into familiar configurations and hence resolutions. Intake workers, accused by some of serving organizational rather than client need, are in a position to either confirm or refute the stereotype of the local-authority social services as a faceless, inhuman, bureaucratic structure, lacking in both sympathy and innovative potential. Being in a front-line operational unit consequently affords the potential to influence clients' initial experiences of the organization. Furthermore, because intake concentrates resources through a single channel, it facilitates the more rational deployment of resources and carries potential as a monitoring device.

A stable intake structure allows for better planned social work intervention in the light of the agency's resources and priorities than when work is taken on on an *ad hoc* basis. The increased continuity afforded by intake teams results in the development of common policy, more consistent relationships with other agencies, and increased uniformity in the handling of cases. It can, therefore, be argued that intake organization is a prerequisite for, rather than a guarantee of, better services.

Stevenson, reporting on the findings of a study of forty area teams, comments: 'we believe the trend may now be away from intake specialization' (Stevenson 1978: 250). She goes on to suggest that many opportunities exist to experiment in the division of work, such as 'crisis' teams (method based); teams dealing with homelessness (problem based); or teams dealing with the handicapped (client-group based).

Goldberg *et al.* (1977), studying one year's intake to an area team, question whether the aims and functions of social services departments should be as all embracing as they are at present, and whether social workers have the requisite skills for all the roles they have to assume. They see the unitary approach as leading the way towards more-appropriate solutions to the problems which confront social services departments; for example, by adopting a group and community approach to work on a new housing development. They also comment that casework as a method of intervention at in-dividual and family level can be most profitably used in the early manifestations of inter-personal and social stress rather than as a last resort in intractable situations. The former, however, are the sort of situations rarely presented to or taken on by intake workers, and consequently by the department. Consequently, they conclude that it would be most advisable to redeploy resources and change methods of work so as to shift the emphasis away from an information/advice and social casualty service towards a more community-orientated preventive endeavour.

The 1960s saw a rapid increase in the number of self-help groups – for example, squatters groups, tenants associations, and play-groups – and a growing interest in the development of community work, largely in response to problems of massive population change. Seebohm foresaw the need for the personal social services to engage in the task of encouraging and assisting the development of com-munity identity and mutual-aid schemes. Community work and social work, although working in the same sphere, have long been uneasy bedfellows, the former concentrating more on the collective, the latter on the individual. By 1975 there was increasing pressure for separate and independent training for community work on the grounds that it was a practice in its own right, not simply traditional social work with a community bias (Younghusband 1978*b*).

Leissner (1977) considers that there are two types of community

work: service delivery community work, which makes the department's services accessible and relevant to the area and develops a
network of services and resources of which the local authority is a
part; and resident-focused community work aimed at helping groups
of residents define their own needs and take action to meet them.
Both are equally important to social services departments who see
themselves as having a broad-based mandate towards their area of
service. The current trend towards patch-based teams within area
teams is based on a philosophy which seeks to focus on the overall
needs of the community served and to take into account the effects
the environment has on individual clients, and consequently
emphasizes the importance of preventive work and the potential for
community participation and social action. Patch-based workers
have a greater opportunity to know their area, resources, and key
people than when working across a larger geographical area, and in
rural areas there is the practical advantage of reducing the time
spent in travelling to visits.

Rigid allocation of work by patch, however, carries the disadvantage that the patch worker has to provide a total service and
there is little possibility of allowing for differentiation of worker
according to the client's problem. In an area where the worker is
well known and identified there is also the question of confidentiality
to be taken into consideration. Patch work basically complies with
Leissner's 'service delivery community work'; it is an attempt to
bring conventional social work closer to clients and to encourage
local participation by using volunteers, helping in the establishment
of community groups, and sometimes sharing of premises.

Parker (1978) writes of social workers having recently become
aware of a 'rediscovered resource' – informal or natural helping
networks of relatives, neighbours, and friends. Such networks are of
particular relevance to care of the elderly at a time of economic
recession and consequent reduction in the expansion of residential
services for the elderly coupled with the 'geriatric explosion'. If the
trends towards combining informal caring networks and the statutory
services is to be fostered, then the latter need to adapt to the former
and identify more closely with geographical neighbourhoods. That
is, organize on a patch basis. Parker, therefore, suggests that rather
than teams collectively working an area, the area should be reduced
to patches with one or two social workers working each, the patch

then being used as the basis for referral allocation. Patch systems based on the philosophy of supporting and mobilizing natural networks rest on a number of assumptions: that most care for dependent groups in the community – for example the elderly, mentally ill, and mentally or physically handicapped – is provided by informal networks of family, friends, and neighbours rather than by statutory services; that people identified as clients in one context often have strengths that make them a valuable resource in other contexts; and that, in general, problems cannot be divorced from the community in which they arise.

The principal role of social services departments, therefore, becomes one of helping to support informal care-givers; encouraging the development of potential in the community to provide mutual aid; developing links with other agencies at grass-roots level; and breaking down barriers between professionals and the community, thereby facilitating access to the whole range of state social services. Because area teams cover relatively large populations, and usually work from centralized offices, they react to problems then prevent them, and problems tend to be conceptualized in personal and individual terms. Advocates of patch systems hold that, to understand and form links with family and neighbourhood networks, organizations must be locally based. A survey carried out by Hadley and McGrath (1979) found that all patch-based teams felt more enmeshed in their local community since working on a local basis and, therefore, felt they were providing a more effective service. The data base for this was the increase in the number of referrals coupled with the gradual decrease in emergency work.

In addition to the current trend towards patch-based teams in social services departments there is also evident a discernible move towards specialist-based teams – that is, social work teams within an area team concentrating on specific client groups, for example the under fives, adolescents, children in long-term care, the mentally disordered, or the elderly. This move is supported by many professionals on the grounds that the advent of generic work has diluted the expertise available to clients, and that no individual worker can realistically be expected to work across the whole range of social service provision. Some teams combine these two strands to form generic teams, with individual workers specializing either formally or informally in work with particular client groups, but working with a particular geographical sub-division of the area's catchment. The question then arises as to whether developments such as these necessarily herald the demise of intake teams. The major drawback of an intake-team operation where there is an area commitment to patch working lies in the area of task demarcation. Long-term teams' knowledge of and participation in a particular neighbour-hood cannot be extended to crisis work, and long-term workers do not necessarily get the 'feel' of the referrals coming in from their patch if these are dealt with by a separate (intake) team. It is also suggested that intake and long-term teams may operate different sets of priorities, although theoretically priority setting should be the task of the area as a whole and, therefore, the same thinking should govern both intake and long-term teams.

If patch teams are to handle their own intake work, this requires a high proportion of staff time being taken up by such work; for example, four patches would require four social workers to be on duty each day. At the same time the amount of time available for non-duty work is reduced. If patch teams rotate covering duty this negates the advantage of each patch taking its own referrals, and is indeed probably disadvantageous – in comparison with intake-team organization – in causing a lack of commitment to referrals outside the worker's own patch and hence a tendency to 'take messages'. Specialist-based teams covering duty share similar problems, possibly more so. For example, because of the range of requests at the point of intake, a social worker specializing in the under fives may have very little knowledge, experience, or expertise in assessing psychogeriatric problems, and the spectre of the confusion and poor level of service offered to clients after Seebohm reorganization looms once more. The intake model is therefore apparently not necessarily inherently in conflict with organization along the lines of patch-based or specialist-based teams, and the many advantages that accrue from the intake model of organization can and should be preserved while allowing developments in organization and practice in directions of both patch participation and specialization.

There is no apparent reason why intake teams, dealing with assessment, crisis, and short-term work, should not relate to other social work teams organized along either patch or specialist lines. As in the intake/long-term model, the degree of open communication between teams is crucial. If patch workers are freed from the

bombardment, at whatever level, with new referrals they theoretically have more time available to include themselves in neighbourhood activities and to undertake preventive work. If communication
between intake and patch workers is positive they act as a mutual
resource; the intake worker may refer a client to a patch worker or
project, or seek advice from the patch team about what relevant
resources are available. Furthermore, many of the advantages
claimed for patch work derive from working with informal networks
to support dependants, many of whom are likely to be long-term
clients anyway. In relation to specialist teams the intake model of
organization would seem to be the only realistic way of handling
incoming work, which would subsequently, after assessment, be
referred to the appropriate specialist worker.

A recent study by Gostick and Scott (1980) found that 46 per cent
of the area teams surveyed had intake teams, and their presence was
not, as may have been expected, confined to inner city and urban
areas. Out of the five counties surveyed, four had made substantial
use of intake teams, and such teams also continued to grow in
counties and metropolitan districts. The data suggested that on
average ten new intake teams were being started each year and the
authors found little evidence of the abandonment of intake teams,
although in some London boroughs there is evidently a change in
the emphasis of long-term teams towards the development of
complementary patch or specialist teams; in a handful of boroughs
intake teams have been disbanded, with an increased focus on patch
work. Intake teams' major expectations of themselves were related
to the efficient and effective handling of work flow, being the
front-line operational unit for the agency. In talking of possible
future developments, they talked of creating better links with
community groups and other organizations, improving their identification with particular neighbourhoods, and with specialist
services for particular client groups. Long-term teams were reported
as keen to improve the system of case transfer, become more
involved in the content of intake work, and to move back into what
they viewed as the 'policy making' part of the area. The authors
conclude:

'Our findings confirm that specialist intake teams are continuing
to thrive despite the emergence of new organizational structures
and the renewal of the debate about specialization. Moreover,

they appear to be facing the 1980s with the same commitment and enthusiasm they brought to the early post-Seebohm departments and enriched by their collective experience of operating in the front line of social service delivery.'

(Gostick and Scott 1980: 22)

If it continues to be the object of local-authority social work to provide a generic social work service to the public, and if social work practice is to continue to change and adapt to the demands made of it and the philosophy that underlies it, adequate assessment and crisis work can be viewed as the essential prerequisite to the provision of an adequate service. Specialist intake teams of social workers with their own particular range of knowledge, skills, and expertise, and with a remit to undertake such work, makes for sound practice not only in terms of organizational efficiency and the effective deployment of staff, but also in relation to the service available to clients and other referring agencies.

References

Austin, L. N. (1965) Foreword. In H. J. Parad (ed.) *Crisis Intervention: Selected Readings*. New York: Family Service Association of America.

Bamford, T. (1977) The changing role of social work. *Social Work Today* **9**: 1.

Barker, P. J. (1975) Clients' likes and dislikes. *Social Work Today* **6**: 77–8.

Barnes, R. (1975) Mau-Mauing the duty officer. *Social Work Today* **6**: 162–65.

Bellak, L. and Small, L. (1965) *Emergency Psychotherapy and Brief Psychotherapy*. New York: Grune and Stratton.

Boucher, R. (1976) The first 12 months of an intake team. *Social Work Today* **8**: 12–13.

British Association of Social Workers (1977) *The Social Work Task – A BASW Working Party Report*. Birmingham: BASW Publications.

Bromley, G. (1978) Grades and specialization in social work practice. *Social Work Today* **10**: 16–23.

Caplan, G. (1964) *Principles of Preventive Psychiatry*. London: Tavistock Publications.

Challis, L. (1974) Taking on intake: Conference report. *Social Services* 9 Feb.: 8.

Cooper, J. (1978) The collective and the personal – a decade of tension. *Community Care* 12 Dec.: 14–15.

Cooper, T. (1979) Growth in the process of helping. *Social Work Today* **11**: 13–14.

Corney, R. (1979) Different styles of intervention. *Social Work Today* **11**: 15–17.

Corrie, E. (1976) Intake: Friend or foe? *Social Work Today* **6**: 713–15.

Day, P., Rhodes, V., and Truefitt, T. (1978) Priorities and an area team. *Social Work Today* **10**: 22–3.

Denham, E. J. M. (1976) *Intake Teams – An Interim Appraisal*. Strathclyde Regional Council Social Work Research Unit. (Unpublished data.)

Department of Health and Social Security (1975) *The Service Delivery Study*. Social Work Service No. 6. London: DHSS.

—— (1978) *Social Service Teams: The Practitioner's View*. London: HMSO.

Duncan, T. M. (1973) Intake in an integrated team. *Health and Social Service Journal* 10 Feb.: 318–19.

Dunn, G. (1978) After Seebohm, the deluge. *Community Care* 13 Dec.: 16–17.

Evans, R. (1978) Unitary models of practice and the social work team. In M. R. Olsen (ed.) *The Unitary Model*. Birmingham University Social Work Studies, Occasional Paper No. 1. Birmingham: BASW Publications.

Frank, J. D. (1973) *Persuasion and Healing: A Comparative Study of Psychotherapy*. Baltimore, Maryland: Johns Hopkins University Press.

Georgiou, A. (1977) *Area Teams: The organization and the social worker*. University of Swansea, applied social studies dissertation. (Unpublished data.)

Gill, O. and Boaden, N. (1976) Training for intake. *Social Work Today* **8**: 9–11.

Glampson, A. and Goldberg, E. M. (1976) Post-Seebohm social services: (2) The consumers' viewpoint. *Social Work Today* **8**: 7–12.

Goldberg, E. M. and Fruin, D. J. (1976) Towards accountability in social work: A case review system for social workers. *British Journal of Social Work* **6**: 3–22.

Goldberg, E. M. and Robinson, J. (1977) An Area Office of an English social services department. In W. J. Reid and L. Epstein (eds) *Task Centred Practice*. New York: Columbia University Press.

Goldberg, E. M., Warburton, R. W., Lyons, L. J., and Willmott, R. W. (1978) Towards accountability in social work: Long-term social work in an area office. *British Journal of Social Work* **8**: 253–87.

204   Intake Teams

Goldberg, E. M., Warburton, R. W., McGuinness, B., and Rowlands, J. H. (1977) Towards accountability in social work: One year's intake to an area office. *British Journal of Social Work* **7**: 257–83.

Gostick, C. (1976) The intake phenomenon. *Social Work Today* **8**: 7–9.

Gostick, C. and Scott, T. (1980) Intake teams – dead or alive? *Community Care* 4 Sept.: 20–2.

Hadley, R. and McGrath, M. (1979) Patch based social services. *Community Care* 11 Oct.: 16–18.

Hall, A. (1975) Policy making: More judgement than luck. *Community Care* 6 Aug.: 16–18.

Hall, A., Glampson, A., and Fruin, D. (1976) Don't call us . . . we'll call you. *Community Care* 4 Feb.: 14–16.

HMSO (1968) *Report on the Committee on Local Authority and Allied Personal Social Services.* Cmnd 3703.

Hutton, J. (1977) *Short-Term Contracts in Social Work.* London: Routledge and Kegan Paul.

Jones, J. W. (1974) The intake group as an alternative service delivery structure. *Health and Social Service Journal* 23 Mar.: 672.

Kaplan, D. M. and Mason, E. A. (1965) Maternal reactions to premature birth viewed as an acute emotional disorder. In H. J. Parad (ed.) *Crisis Intervention: Selected Readings.* New York: Family Service Association of America.

Langsley, D. G., Slomeuhast, K., and Machotka, P. (1971) Avoiding mental hospital admissions – a follow-up study. *American Journal of Psychiatry* **127**: 1391–394.

Leissner, A. (1977) Social action and political realities. *Social Work Today* **9**: 22–5.

Liddiard, R. (1978) Will America go Seebohm? *Community Care* 13 Dec.: 18–19.

Loewenstein, C. (1974) An intake team in action in a social services department. *British Journal of Social Work* **4**: 115–41.

Malan, D. G. (1963) *A Study of Brief Psychotherapy.* London: Tavistock Publications.

Marsh, N. (1974) Teamwork and social work practice. *Health and Social Service Journal* 30 Mar.: 726–27.

Mayer, J. E. and Timms, N. (1970) *The Client Speaks.* London: Routledge and Kegan Paul.

Neill, J. E., Warburton, R. W., and McGuinness, B. (1976) Post-

Seebohm social services: (1) The social worker's viewpoint. *Social Work Today* **8**: 9–14.

Neill, J. E., Fruin, D., Goldberg, E. M., and Warburton, R. W. (1973) Reactions to integration. *Social Work Today* **4**: 458–65.

Olsen, M. R. (ed.) (1978) *The Unitary Model*. Birmingham University Social Work Studies, Occasional Paper No. 1. Birmingham: BASW Publications.

Oriss, H. D. (1974) A local social service. *Health and Social Service Journal* 2 Nov.: 2542.

Parad, H. J. (1976) Crisis intervention in mental health emergencies: Theory and technique in work with the emotionally disturbed and and mentally disordered. In M. R. Olsen (ed.) *Differential Approaches in Social Work with the Mentally Disordered*. BASW Occasional Papers No. 2. Birmingham: BASW Publications.

Parker, P. (1978) Reaching out to a wider network. *Community Care* 18 Oct.: 21–2.

Perlman, H. H. (1960) Intake and some role considerations. *Social Casework* **41**: 171–77.

—— (1970) The problem-solving model in social casework. In R. W. Roberts and R. H. Nee (eds) *Theories of Social Casework*. Chicago: University of Chicago Press.

Personal Social Services Council (1976) *Social Services Manpower Resources*. London: PSSC.

Prodgers, A. (1979) Defences against stress in intake work. *Social Work Today* **11**: 12–14.

Rapoport, L. (1970) Crisis intervention as a mode of brief treatment. In R. W. Roberts and R. H. Nee (eds) *Theories of Social Casework*. Chicago: University of Chicago Press.

Rapp, D. (1974) Learning to say No. *Health and Social Service Journal* 30 Mar.: 728.

Rees, S. (1974) No more than contact: An outcome of social work. *British Journal of Social Work* **4**: 255–79.

Reid, W. J. (1977) Task-centred treatment and trends in clinical social work. In W. J. Reid and L. Epstein (eds) *Task Centred Practice*. New York: Columbia University Press.

Reid, W. J. and Shyne, A. W. (1969) *Brief and Extended Casework*. New York: Columbia University Press.

Reith, D. (1975) I wonder if you can help me . . .? *Social Work Today* **6**: 66–9.

Sainsbury, E. and Nixon, S. (1979) Approaching the Welfare. *Social Work Today* **10**: 16–19.

Scott, T. (1974) *Intake systems – an interim appraisal.* National Institute of Social Work discussion paper. (Unpublished data.)

Seebohm, F. (1977) Lord Seebohm speaks: The Seebohm reorganization – what went wrong? *Social Work Today* **9**: 10–11.

Shaw, M. (1979) Social work revisited. *Community Care* 5 April: 15–17.

Shearer, A. (1979) Society tomorrow: Sir George throws down the challenge. *The Guardian* 10 Oct.

Smith, G. and Ames, J. (1976) Area teams in social work practice: A programme for research. *British Journal of Social Work* **6**: 43–69.

Social Services Organization Research Unit (1974) *Social Services Departments.* Brunel Institute of Organization and Social Studies. London: Heinemann.

Spencer, C. (1973) Support as a key position in social work. *Social Work Today* **3**: 4–7.

Stevenson, O. (1977) Focus on the task of the local-authority social worker. *Social Work Today* **9**: 11–14.

—— (1978) Seebohm – seven years on. *New Society* **43**: 249–51.

Streatfield, D. (1979) Information – making the system work. *Social Work Today* **10**: 10–12.

Streatfield, D. and Mullings, C. (1979) *Communicating Information in Social Services Departments.* Social Work Service No. 20.

Titcomb, B. (1974) Setting up an intake team. *Community Care* 26 Aug.

Vickery, A. (1973) Specialist: Generic: What next? *Social Work Today* **4**: 262.

—— (1977) Use of unitary models in education for social work. In H. Specht and A. Vickery (eds) *Integrating Social Work Methods.* National Institute Social Services Library No. 31. London: Allen and Unwin.

Wetton, K. (1976) The Cheltenham intake team: An evaluation. Clearing House for Local Authority Social Services Research, University of Birmingham: 1–78.

Wooton, B. (1978) The social work task today. *Community Care* 4 Oct.: 14–15.

Younghusband, E. (1978*a* and *b*) *Social Work in Britain: 1950–75. A follow-up study.* Volumes 1 and 2. London: Allen and Unwin.

Name index

Subject index

accessibility, 16, 30–1, 126
Acts, 129; Children *1948*, 12; Children and Young Person's *1963*, 7, 12, 111; *1969*, 13, 26, 38; Children's *1975*, 134; Chronically Sick and Disabled Persons *1970*, 13, 26, 38, 129; Local Authority Social Services *1971*, 5; Mental Health *1959*, 12, 35, 38, 65; Poor Law, 7, 9
administration, 31, 33, 54, 183
advisers, 133–34
ageing *see* elderly
aims and objectives, 16–23, 75, 164, 185, 194, 196
'Applications Sector', 10
area teams: advantages and disadvantages of, 42–4; establishment of, 6, 28–35, 198; restructuring of, 36–62
assessment, 49, 66–7, 103–05, 153, 168, 188, 193, 199
Association of Child Care Officers, 11
Association of Psychiatric Social Workers, 11
attachment schemes, 91–2

basic-grade worker, 189
BASW *see* British Association of Social Workers
boundaries, 27, 122
Brief and Extended Casework, 158, 205
British Association of Social Workers, 46, 176, 191, 202

British Medical Association, 6
Brunel team, 10

'case-based' work, 167
caseload, 78–84, 90
casework, 9–10, 141–45, 158, 166, 196
'casualty' basis of service, 17–18
categorization, premature, 87, 175, 195; *see also* mis-referrals
charities *see* voluntary organizations
'Child, The Family and the Young Offender, The', 12
childminding, 15
children, 7–14, 26, 38–9, 111, 134–37, 142, 179–82
Children Act *1948*, 12
Children and Young Persons Act: *1963*, 7, 12, 111; *1969*, 13, 26, 38
Children's Act *1975*, 134
Children's Departments, 8–11, 14, 39, 142
Chronically Sick and Disabled Person's Act *1970*, 13, 26, 38, 129
Citizens Advice Bureau, 55, 91, 117–18, 121, 180; *see also* organizations, other
Claimants Union, 101
classification of problems, 43
'clearing-house' function, 187
clerical functions of intake, 40, 42, 45, 54, 141; *see also* receptionists
client-group work, 142, 146, 173–74, 188, 190, 196

Supplementary Benefits: Commission, 11; Tribunal, 65, 121
support from colleagues *see* communication
surveillance, 79, 111, 162–63

task-centred treatment, 160–63
teachers, 18
teamwork, 73–7
telephone calls, 52
telephonists, 35, 52, 88; *see also* receptionists
tenants associations, 18–19, 196
tertiary prevention, 149
time, 25; -limited crises, 151–55; rationing, 126
training: community work, 196; generic, 21, 165, 171, 187, 191–92; post-qualification, 25, 191; social work, 20–1, 39; specialist, 171
transfer from intake, 82–4; difficulties of, 182–84, 200; variables affecting, 176–80

unification of social services, 5–35; *see also* Seebohm Report
uniformity, 94–100, 195; *see also* consistency
unitary model, 165–70
United States, 32; casework in, 141, 143, 158; and crisis intervention, 141;

mental illness in, 156; organization problems in, 16; task-centred approach in, 161; unitary model in, 166, 169

voluntary organizations, 7, 11, 29, 117, 121, 137, 139; *see also* organizations, other

Welfare Department, 11, 24, 78, 142
White Paper *1965*, 12
work: allocation of, 57–62; nature of, 85–113
workers: associations, 11, 46, 176, 191, 202; and clients, relationship, 30–1; communication between, 31, 33, 61, 74, 76, 111, 118, 130–31, 138, 181–83, 199–200; as diagnosticians, 176; expectations, 107; goals, 164, 185; information needs of, 129–34; numbers of, 23–4, 77, 177, 183; output, increase, 47; personal preferences of, 126–27; personality of, 110; roles of, 90–1, 108, 111, 117, 140, 153, 161, 169, 172–73, 177–78, 200; senior, 53, 76, 95, 111, 183; skills of, 21, 46–7, 55–6, 75, 138–39, 165, 168, 170, 179, 188–89; stress of, 74, 109–11; training, 20–1, 25, 165, 171, 187, 191–92, 196